½ WAYS TO MAKE A GIRL FALL FOR YOU

Cyrus Broacha, the most famous MTV VJ, is also a beloved stand-up comedian and noted prankster. Best known for his show *Bakra*, Cyrus also anchored a hugely popular news satire show, *The Week That Wasn't*, co-written and directed by friend Kunal Vijayakar.

23½ WAYS TO MAKE A GIRL FALL FOR YOU

CYRUS BROACHA

Published by
Rupa Publications India Pvt. Ltd 2016
7/16, Ansari Road, Daryaganj
New Delhi 110002

Sales Centres:

Allahabad Bengaluru Chennai
Hyderabad Jaipur Kathmandu
Kolkata Mumbai

Copyright © Cyrus Broacha 2016

The views and opinions expressed in this book are the author's own and the facts are as reported by him which have been verified to the extent possible, and the publishers are not in any way liable for the same.

All rights reserved.
No part of this publication may be reproduced, transmitted, or stored in a retrieval system, in any form or by any means, electronic, mechanical, photocopying, recording or otherwise, without the prior permission of the publisher.

ISBN: 978-81-291-3957-3

First impression 2016

*To Mikhail, Maya, my parents Farrokh and Olivia,
my wife Ayesha.
And to my beloved Ruffo,
till we meet again this side of heaven.*

The people at Rupa—apparently there are 38,563 of them (although most are freelancers and at least one is a six-year-old)—were very clear.

'We need you to write us a book'. One of them nonchalantly mentioned, I think it was the tall one, though it may have been the squat one, standing behind the tall one. I can't quite recall. My response, as always, to anyone who says 'write a book', is to cry. Weep copiously, and beg to be placed in ice-cold water, in order to feel less anxiety, apprehension and pain.

In the interest of getting to the point in the next three days or so, let me tell you that the people at Rupa had done their homework. Thus, eliciting a quick, compassionate response from nerdy eleven-year-old school girls who always copied down all the notes, and finished their homework in time.

They had read all my earlier works, and were particularly

knees seemed to have said. No it was the one with the unibrow! Actually now that you mention it, it was the squat guy standing behind the tall guy. I'm pretty much 20 per cent sure. I think.

Anyway, Rupa and I have come to an understanding based on facts. First—regardless of spellings I use my right hand. Second—although I asked for crores of rupees as remuneration, they agreed to pay me in handshakes. And if Ebola dies down, occasionally in hugs. Third—I won't miss my deadline by more than a year. Fourth—I will write *23½ Ways To Make a Girl*
Even though I personally have used only 16 ways myself. Mostly to no effect. Fifth—if the Mahila Mandal office, situated directly opposite the Rupa office insists (by frequently and rightfully pelting stones at the Rupa office), then I must keep another version of the same book handy for publication,
23½ Ways To Make a Boy Fall for You. Even though, here too I've personally employed only sixteen ways. However, with far better results!

Lastly, if this book wins the Man Booker Prize, they (Rupa) will pay for my train journey to and from the country of England. If instead, it causes me to win the Noble Peace Prize, I undertake to bear all costs to Sweden by myself.

Since, dear reader, this introduction has casually lost its way, I spoke to the guy from (Rupa), with the hairless legs, agreement, and that forthwith. I begin this book with another introduction, to be called 'Re-Introduction'. Never in the history of human literary writings has such an onerous task been attempted. Woody Allen thought about it. Dave Barry almost attempted it, but for a stomach bug. Arthur Miller tweeted about doing it, sadly just one hour before his untimely death.

Yet, be that as it may, I will be the first author to ever carry a re-introduction. So join me, dear reader, on this… err… historic occasion, by reading the epic, monumental re-introduction to follow. This should be done by touching your right ear to your right shoulder, and reading without complaining.

re-introduction

Why a book on helping Indian men find love?

Two reasons. First, the *Kama Sutra* has failed. Second, according to a study done by W.H.O. (World Health Organization), the Indian male suffers from the most serious case of S.A.G. (Social Awkwardness & Guilt). I will elaborate more about S.A.G., a little later. But in case you are trying to find the W.H.O. document, let me tell you frankly, I seem to have misplaced it. And, mysteriously no carbon print or shadow of it seems to be available now at the present time, which is ten minute after lunch, today.

The Indian male approaches women with mostly great trepidation, and even horror. He traditionally has no game. He will occasionally offset this, by over-compensating and acting overconfident around women. But this is all bluster, and in 70 per cent of all cases, the overconfident one has secretly wet connect with the opposite sex. You all must have attended 'that' party. 'That' party, is the one where you have 125 men dancing with each other, feverishly, while the seventeen women at the do look on, less than spellbound. These, mind you, are all heterosexual men, yet they form a mob, and then pretty soon enact a dance frenzy, all sans the ladies. You think this would happen in Naples? Such behaviour is unheard of in Rio de Janeiro. And in Crimea if 125 men are dancing with each other, shootings will be inevitable. So on God's green earth, only in India does this phenomena occur. All the time, as we speak… err… okay as I write and you speak.

Then there's that great paradox—similar to North Korea calling herself a democracy. But, with far worse implications. Only in India will you see men walking, holding each other's hand whilst ogling at the ladies. They check the women out, mouths agape, pupils dilated in the time-honoured tradition of the village lout, but lo and behold, whilst always, always holding each other's hands, tenderly.

So, dear reader, I have pulled up my forty-three years of experience, spent watching and observing the Indian male at play. I quite rightfully call myself the foremost authority on him. I know his look, his odour, his language, his mannerisms, and you may not believe this but if you put him in a line with

As such this lonely, socially inept, gross failure of a species, is my N.G.O. My 'cause non célèbre'!

Someone has to help uplift the socially downtrodden. I feel that someone is 'moi'.

In the following pages, I try to find help and assistance for this helpless, abjectly socially poor group, who clearly should be given 'special Tribal status'. The underdeveloped socially-bereft Indian male—this book is for you!

Let's begin with the case of Abhishek and Neha. Although, I wanted to start with Bhanumathi and Priyanshu. But apparently we don't have the rights, even though Bhanumathi and Priyanshu are a figment of my imagination. So, Abhishek and Neha it is. And in that sentence alone lies the crux of this issue.

In this sentence itself India's sexism and gender bias has been exposed. The root of the male social failure and apathy in India may well reside in the sentence. You see, in calling the case study as Abhishek and Neha, we have elevated the male name into the first place. Subconsciously, lording Abhishek's madness and confusing Neha to the secondary position. This is the fundamental issue I have with the Indian male. Granted, along with his stand against flossing and his love for gargling with sound effects, in public places.

The day we subconsciously refer to this case study as Neha and Abhishek, writing this book becomes redundant. I was hoping that day would be next Tuesday, but inside information that has mysteriously fallen into my lap, sideways says it most

In the west it's always Bonnie & Ctyde. In the west of India, however, no one has ever heard of Bonnie. C'est la vie!

To trace the genius of this 'sexism complex' leads to loud arguments, mostly those one has with oneself. Does something happen during conception? Pre-conception? In the womb? Does the male get offered the bigger breast while feeding? The possibilities are endless? And, in the next seven books on this subject, we'll examine each and every theory.

But here's the thing. In actuality, there is no Abhishek and Neha. You see Abhishek mistakenly thinks there's a Neha, but she hasn't even met him yet. To understand more, let's go straight to Abhishek's letter. This letter was written to an agony aunt. Which is very different to the dramatically ungrammatically, 'a' agony aunt. For misplaced reasons, that aunt was me. I know, don't ask. Don't know. No! Never! Let me instead introduce

> I'm seeing a girl called Neha, and I'm seeing her every day at the bus stop, but she is not seeing me. Today she was wearing a green T-shirt and blue jeans with blue shoes. Yesterday it was yellow shoes, blue jeans and a yellow shirt. I stand directly behind her at the bus stop, but she hasn't

23½ Ways to Make a Girl Fall For You

you, she went green. I am scared to talk to her owing to one particular incident. Last week I poked her back with my umbrella. She glared at me so I pretended it was an

How do I get her to notice me? One more thing, I can't keep standing at this bus stop, because it isn't my stop. So can you please help me to marry her?

Yours sincerely,
Abhishek N.
a.k.a. The Kool Rider

This letter is the classic case of sadly the deluded Indian romantic male, who has no 'game'. Mistakenly, the better socially acquainted like to call such a person 'shameless'. That would be incorrect. Such a person is not 'shameless', he's gameless! He has no strategy to woo. And if he does, it's a ridiculously ineffective one invoking, I dare say, an umbrella

So what advice do you give such a lamentable fellow? Well, it's all there in my contrite reply.

Dear Abhishek,

First off, I hope you haven't been arrested! No seriously,

is doing at the stop is a point worth considering. By the contents of your letter, I gather that you have not really interacted with the opposite sex. But of all the ridiculously stupid things to do in order to gain female attention, your attempt to colour-coordinate takes the cake. The last male to successfully pull off yellow shoes in public, was Mr Michael Jackson. And by all accounts he didn't have a great record with the ladies. Though he did have some really great records especially when heard from a

Your performance in romance is like an infant's in a library of Greek classics. Provided the infant isn't Virgil himself, of course, who wouldn't be pulled out of the library by ten dead horses.

Here are my three basic steps for you to peruse:

> You are not seeing a girl, until you are both mutually dating each other of your own free will.
> Always start with a simple conversation. 'Hello' works fine. 'What's up' doesn't always sound right in a thick Indian accent.
> Loud clothes, loud gestures, loud movements scare off ladies immediately, unless they are a meter away,

Please, please get rid of your umbrella. Also stop going to her bus stop, and find some genuine common meeting ground. Dress like you used to, before you saw your 'love interest', and begin with a simple 'Hi'.

It worked for the great Bob Marley although he took things to another level. Your first step is just a friendly greeting. Yellow shoes are to be used only twenty-five years after marriage when you want to rid yourself of your partner, your friends and all types of flora and fauna.

Yours hesitatingly,
XYZ

This first article sets the pace for our monumental thesis which luckily is neither this particularly cerebral book, nor in fact the next one. In all probability it's the seventh one down the line. This letter is important to set up the standard of the Indian men who are hopelessly at sea in their quest

A Wooing Woman Index by the W.W.O. (the World Wooing Organization) ranks India at 177 out of 187 countries. And bear in mind two of the countries ranked below us have ceased to exist—Crete and North Western Somalia.

There are many ways to address the issue. At a young age,

the ladies. The Black Bear is painfully shy, yet quite successful in courtship. And the caterpillar really goes the extra yard, a distance which normally takes him, a whole day.

Now back to the Indian males, all of the above can be used as guiding tools, but only if we create the actual, factual surroundings in which he may be forced to deal with the opposite sex. But before I spell out the scenarios let's look at the three basic Indian male personality types. There are, according to Singh and Souza, 'The Masculine Men of Mathura', in their
159 Different Personality Types amongst Males. But since I couldn't get past page seven of their book, let's stick to just three, who were very clearly depicted along with pictures, by page five-and-a-half .

The first type, which we will call Type A, is the shy and retiring type. This one is perennially afraid of social contact. And can't bring himself to even talk to the other gender. Normally, this would be a quality women would appreciate the most. But Mr Shy is perhaps the most difficult one to mould into a 'lady

Type A by its very presence creates Type B. This is the antithesis of Type A. He is overfriendly and overbearing with the opposite sex. Although not dangerous, he has no plan and comes on too strong. This is the easiest type to work with, as

And now armed with this very important half-baked piece of information, let us look at all the various scenarios where the genders would collide. Bear in mind all these varied options are based on seventeen years of exhaustive research using a pan-India team of over 160 people, or three Hindi films, I can't

The Art of Introduction

'Introduction' is an English word which has gone into the Indian lexicon as Intro. There is no parallel in our regional languages. If two people are speaking in chaste Bengali, and one requests the other to introduce him to a girl, then the word 'intro' has to be used. This is a very powerful word in gender interactivity. A good 'intro', is half the battle. Other popular English words adopted by India with a twist in the meaning include 'Baba' and 'Tata'. In English, 'Baba' is just a clear case of stammering. In India, it refers to a young male of some consequence. Very often the 'Baba' is the protagonist in the 'intro' episode. 'Tata', on the other hand, refers to a popular dance form in Merry Olde England. To dance the Tatas. In India, it's very often used as a way of signalling farewell. Very often to the 'Baba', who impudently had set and then some, this has been the first step in meeting a member of the opposite sex. Sadly, very often it also was the last step.

Who hasn't been asked to help out with an 'intro'? If there be one amongst you, speaketh now or forever hold your peace.

Picture a busy day in a city college. Girls rushing about their business amongst frightened boys, who stare as if they are in a trance, feet moving less then Virendar Sehwag's. The boys are trapped like rabbits in front of headlights. As the women volume lessens, the boys start looking for answers. They find solace amongst each other. As they acknowledge each other's helplessness, they also start comparing notes. Words like 'hot', 'super-hot', 'chest', 'derriere' and 'smoking hot' fill the air. It is then, in this haze of a new dawn, one they are ill prepared for, that favorites are marked out. Some liked the girls in red. Some the yellow dupatta. The less weird ones like the girl 'out' of the yellow dupatta. While preferences are being bandied about, a common realization affects the entire cadre. And that is the value of an introduction. This small step for man, is a gigantic, humongous, enormous leap for the male teenager (who will forever remain a teenager).

Here, is a quick concise guide to the rules of the introduction. These rules are shrouded in secrecy and should be committed to memory and then thrown away. These rules have come to

Get an introduction to a girl you are interested in, by someone who knows the girl, which also translates into someone who the girl knows as well.

When introduced, make sure your real name is used, i.e., if your name is Mahindra, but your pet name is 'Soda', please don't be introduced as a soft drink. It may leave a lasting impression, but not necessarily the right one.

Have a valid reason for the introduction, like taking a ride together, or raising money for a college event, and not because you've been staring at her for the last 7.15 hours without blinking even once.

At the time of the introduction, please don't ask for her phone number, and don't ask her if she's on Facebook. Assume that she is, and at this point in her life she doesn't want to drop everything to 'friend' you.

Don't ask her out immediately. You've been introduced to her, you haven't married her. (Of course, that brings us to couples who got married and wished they had been introduced first. But that's a whole other book.)

Next day, don't go tom-toming on the internet that you made your first kill. Save Twitter for more intimate details of your life, like when did you go to the toilet last and the college gate and give her a decent, not too exuberant, not too familiar or invasive, 'Hello'.

♥

In short, the introduction can best be summed up by the final lines Casablanca, 'This could be the beginning of a

And now, dear reader, let's start our friendship. Based loosely on the penship and pain of letter writers in love from all over. In each successive letter they tell me of their travails, their challenges, their anguish, and sometimes, only sometimes, I pretend to listen. So, let's keep an open mind, and more importantly try not to fall asleep in the next few pages. And by few pages, I mean, just five.

♥

I have fallen for a girl called Nazneen. We live in the same area. Her building is three buildings away from mine. We meet near the local paan-wallah, where I buy and smoke a cigarette from time to time. If she's passing at the same time, I wave to her. Of the twenty-seven occasions I've waved to her, she's waved back. Once I thought it was told me never to wave at Nazneen again. I decided to keep it casual, so I hardly said a word. Also, I was being asphyxiated at the same time, so I needed to prioritize basic breathing at this juncture. However, I read somewhere that if the girl's relatives threaten you it means she definitely likes you. So Sir, should I see this as a positive sign? Should I approach her from the paan-wallah's shop next time? What about the brothers? Please kindly advice?

Yours sincerely,
Ayaz Nalwallah

Let me be straightforward and say if you are four years old, then your letter makes perfect sense. However, if you are older than four, I fear that your mental faculties may not be working at full throttle.

First I need to know where you read this theory that if the relatives threaten you, it means the girl likes you! Was it in a book? Was it on a pamphlet distributed by your building society? Was it on the wall of a public urinal that you frequent?

Do you have a copy of this 'scientific' principle that you espouse, with the name and references of the authors?

urinal as quickly as possible.

Ayaz, if you waved at her twenty-seven times, on twenty-seven different occasions, and possibly got a response only once, the odds are stacked heavily against you, if she has organized some street intimidation (as romantic as that idea may be). It seems pretty clear to me, an independent observer, who has never even visited your building society, or preferred urinal, that the woman probably associates you with the common housefly. That is you are a nuisance, from the world of pestilence. Ayaz, I'm not a big fan of waving to a girl who doesn't know you at all, and certainly not twenty-seven times. At twenty-five, you should have got the message, and stopped. One bad habit at the paan-wallah, would be bad enough.

While there is no harm in approaching a girl in a polite way, you need to learn how to accept rejection. It's not such a bad thing. Even Leonardo DiCaprio and Brad Pitt have faced rejection. In Brad Pitt's case, it was rejection from a famous club of which I'm a member. So don't feel bad. But let this one go.

Yours sincerely,
Sir

23½ Ways to Make a Girl Fall For You

I love a girl with all my heart from Standard VI. I am in Standard X right now and confessed my love to her when I was in the IXth. She had said that she loved me, but as a good friend. At that time she also had a boyfriend. Currently, she's stopped talking to me for some reason. I can't live without her. Please help.

Yours sincerely,
Noel Yash

Now, before I answer please understand that this is another recurring instant, like an amorous female mosquito. I speak, of course, of the 'I can't live without her' diktat. After several glasses of Feni, here came the reply.

The only way I can help you is if the girl has failed at least five times. You see, on an average a ninth standard girl is about fourteen years old, so I need her to have failed at least five times so that she is above the legal age of eighteen. However, if you promise me that this is an 'innocent' relationship, let's proceed. Promise? No answer,

I think you are barking up the wrong tree, stroking the wrong ball, wearing the wrong size of pant... etc. etc. I say learn to live without her and focus and prioritize on the right things for a boy of your age, for instance scratching.

Yours faithfully,

Cyrus

♥

I have a very interesting question for you. I would like to know what the prerequisites for attracting a mate are. I am five foot five years old and weigh sixty-two kilos. I have a steady job at an insurance firm, but I lack the confidence and experience in the area of attracting members of the opposite sex. Could you guide me with a few contrite steps in the right direction in simple English please? I have asked this question to many agony aunt columns but am yet to get a satisfactory reply. So please look at this letter as a personal challenge to yourself. You come highly recommended, so while I don't want to put unnecessary pressure on you, I do need to clarify that I'm expecting something special, thanks to your outstanding work in

23½ Ways to Make a Girl Fall For You

From your self-evaluation I can see that you should have been a long distance runner. Which, by the way, is a profession that attracts many members of the opposite sex in droves. First, thanks for understanding the pressure we writers go through daily. An agony aunt has a huge responsibility. You can't just drop a shawl over your shoulders, powder your hair, and then turn up. You need to help impressionable minds through a whole gamut of life changing decisions—from waxing their legs, to downloading naked pictures of oneself. So your empathy is very well-received by my minor, but proud community of men, who double up as helpful aunts. However, after being so sensitive, you then exert overbearing pressure on me by saying you are expecting something extra special from me! This is causing me to sweat and break out in hives. So please un-send that last request as soon as possible.

Now, coming to your question, which is how to attract members of the opposite sex? My boy, simply put there are many routes you could take. For instance, you could become a famous film star or sportsperson. Apparently girls will then flock to you. You could also simply attract completely—you can try an old-fashioned, largely untested option of promoting yourself in an un-zealous like fashion, whereby your best qualities are highlighted in a charming and non-overtly manner. In other words, the opposite of a matrimonial ad that gives height, weight, complexion and profession as the greatest qualities of the candidate.

You need to perhaps spread yourself around. Avail of opportunity. But there's a fine line between availing and being a creep. So avail carefully. For instance, you meet a colleague in a lift which is crowded, please don't avail. That would freak her out. You can't ask her out on a date in this claustrophobic, public environment. Also, gauge when you can steer a conversation towards socializing. Discuss a movie that you've seen, if she's enthusiastic you may get an opportunity to ask her out for another movie. Again, don't do this in a crowded elevator, or a ladies toilet, or a colleague's funeral.

Soorjit, your height and weight are inconsequential, unless you want to become a jockey. You need to find the 'YOU'. The 'YOU', you like, i.e., the 'YOU' you like that's you. Then avail away.

Yours faithfully,
Sir Cyrus

am twenty-two years of age and I am suffering from hair loss. In the sense that there is nothing left, so I'm clinging to my eyebrows. A doctor prescribed me Dutasteride and Finasteride tablets. After three months my eyebrows have grown, and my nose hair is plentiful. But my biggest problem is that my libido has gone down! I don't feel a strong physical drive for women, like I used to. The other day, I was in Ferguson's college, attending a seminar, but in spite of the hall being filled with pretty women, I fell asleep. As a consequence, I was asked to leave the seminar. Worse, as I was being escorted out, I noticed hair on my hands, on the palms! The downside is that I've started feeling like a primate. I'm losing interest in most things. What can you suggest that will give me back my spirit, my libido, and my life? I don't take alcohol and I'm never visiting a pharmacy again, please help.

Yours faithfully,
Prakash Sai

You are so damn right! Please avoid pharmacies. They can be quite the lottery. And please honestly tell me how many lotteries have you won so far? Fifty? Twenty-seven?

the same time tested the ways it's meant to be treated. By simply wearing a cap and avoiding public showers. Those drugs you mentioned do affect the libido, and the double whammy of extra hair, anywhere but on the head. And in the 44º Celsius Pune heat, doesn't help either.

Please consult a doctor to reverse the effects of these drugs. A helpful hint is to choose a doctor with a head full of hair, and not extremely hairy hands. If he has a hot secretary/nurse, as well as a lecherous leer, even safer.

And now for some good news. Love and lust for the female form is so hardwired into the male DNA that we can get aroused in the most indelicate of situations. Like, when a terrorist group is holding you at ransom, or a death ceremony is being performed. Or even when you are right gab-smacked in the middle of an earthquake, or a tsunami! There are so many recorded cases of death row inmates whose final request would generally be for the complete 'works' of Pamela Anderson. Or Paris Hilton's holistic, contribution to world cinema!

The point is just like General McArthur, your libido will return. And you will have plenty of awkward, wretched, shameful moments with the opposite sex to look forward to in the foreseeable future. So don't worry,

23½ Ways to Make a Girl Fall For You

♥

Myself Omesh Hilwala. I don't know if you can help me but let me tell you my story anyway. I'm seventy-four years of age. About three years ago, my wife of over forty years passed away. I feel now I'm ready to get back in the saddle and hit the dating scene again. I say again only because it sounds hip. In truth, I had an arranged marriage, and prior to that never went on a single date, except when I was sixteen and went out with Nandini to see the movie *Gone with the Wind*. But Nandini's brother ditched last minute, so I and Nandini were forced to go together.

But since we sat in separate rows, I don't know if it counts as a date. Anyway, Nandini passed five years ago, although her brother is still available. But since *Gone with* is not playing anywhere, at this time, the whole thing would be quite futile.

So, young man, where do I begin? To somewhat quote that beautiful movie *Love Story*. Of course, I later watched , with Nandini's brother Kishore, but by then Nandini was already much married, and had seen the

May I say that I find your name a little incomplete? Shouldn't it be 'Romesh' or even 'Promesh'? Omesh sounds like something is missing, if you don't mind my saying so.

But sir, I do find your stars fascinating. And I must applaud you for your vigour at age seventy-four. I mean sitting through the entire film *Love Story*, and that too with another grown man by your side is quite an unparalleled feat! Worthy of some sort of public recognition, at the

However, at seventy-four, you need more of dating website for seniors, to help you in your search for love. And bear in mind, your search is by no means limited to seniors. One can't really imagine you in your seventy-fifth year, chatting up girls at a bus stop. Or chilling in the gym sauna with a bevy of beauties for company. A scene, which I may add, would have made, even *Love Story* bearable, if

The internet and your telephone book, would be the best way to go. I would try and tag an appropriate website, and possibly post an ad with all your considerable assets solidly underlined. Which I think should include your

23½ Ways to Make a Girl Fall For You

you not avail of the same facilities? But remember 64 per cent of these respondents turn out to be frauds. Often they are of the same gender as you, and very often they may also be card-carrying communists, who don't believe

Having said that, your positive outlook leaves me to believe that you will win this war. If I was a girl, my knees would be shaking vigorously by now.

Your semi-truthfully,
C.B.

♥

I am karate expert. A sensei of some repute, I am twenty-nine years of age. I weigh seventy-four kilos, and stand tall at five feet ten inches. I have won sixteen national karate competitions, and I can break six planks of wood with one hand. Recently a student of mine has shown interest in me. She's an amateur car rally driver. Just to keep her happy, I said I also like racing cars! Last week she invited me to participate in a rally outside Faridabad, Haryana, and I said yes! That brings me to my

As of now I have five days to go before the rally. What should I do? I really like this girl. If I come clean, she may be completely turned off? Please help?

Asmit Jhunjhunwalla

It was Carl Jung's cousin Hemlata Jung Balsekar (Balsekar after marriage of course), who spoke about the miracle of positive thinking. She gave various examples, such as the man who raised a car with mind power alone, to save his wife who was trapped under it. Only to realize that he has raised the wrong car. Apparently he got the last two digits mixed up. It wasn't a '17', but a '71', in actuality. By the time he rectified his mistake, and we are talking sixteen cars here, it was too late.

However, your radiant positivity is absolutely exhilarating, as well as befuddling. You are actually asking me whether you should come clean? The alternative being, you take part in a car rally, with super competent passionate professionals, as your competitors, for three consecutive days, along the rural landscape of Haryana, without actually knowing how to drive? This is the equivalent of fifteen days to master. I say enroll in a school now, make some excuse for this weekend, (Asthmatic Bronchitis, a dying relative or my dog ate my home work, are all good) and learn driving as quickly as you can. Then you'll be ready for the next rally. And Asmit, please keep in mind that I applaud your right to lie. But next time you lie, remember to do it with honour, ... and errm... a little intelligent research!

Coming to the second part of your problem, luckily for you I have an old Honda City, lying around somewhere and although the market price for this ten-year-old is ninety-thousand rupees, in light of your desperate situation, I'll let you have it for two lakhs ten thousand only, all inclusive. See, every cloud has a silver lining. So join a motor school, and start coughing now.

Yours helpfully,
C.B.

♥

Dear Uncle Cyrus,

I am eighteen and the girl I loved recently moved to Gujarat. She loves me a lot, though I'm not sure if she concentrate on my studies. How do I know if she is still really interested? Please help me Uncle Cyrus.

Yours sincerely,
Anuj Mathers

First of all, minus two points for calling me 'Uncle'. Second, Gujarat is just three hours away, I say go and have it out. Long distance relationships are tough. Frankly, that's why I gave up both Angelina Jolie and Jennifer Anniston, on a more personal note. But in today's day and age, Gujarat is hardly 'long distance'. Mumbai–Gujarat takes as much time as South Mumbai to Malad in peak evening traffic. So don't be geographically challenged, go to Gujarat. And while you are there, see if you can, pack me some dhoklas from 'Mannibhai's'.

Yours faithfully,
'Uncle' Cyrus

And now we switch genders, just for variety. Let's hear a female voice, even if it's in a deep baritone.

23½ Ways to Make a Girl Fall For You

This happens even more when he's agitated which is a constant state these days.

And then he's got this habit of walking ahead of me in public. He seems to disregard my presence. Last week, we went to a party at the Swaminathans, and he left me behind at the party. Simply forgot to take me back home. He's not forgetful by nature. He's never forgotten to drop himself home, not once. And it's not like he's completely uncaring. The other day when I rang the front door bell, he almost opened the door. But just at the last second, he got a call from his parent company, in New York, and obviously had to attend to it. Luckily, the maid showed up in a couple of hours, so I finally got in, as he's given her a house key.

Ours was an arranged marriage but Mr Rashidi has definitely got some good qualities, none of which come to mind, as of right now. However I want this marriage to work, so what do you think I should do? Here is a list of his qualities, which I'll share with you if it helps matters at all. (a) He's short tempered; (b) He's short; (c) He drools; (d) He's obstinate; (e) He's self-centred; (f) He's always right; (g) He's not altruistic at all; and (h) He never answers me, ever.

Judging by your letter, and I'm hazarding an educated guess here, he seems to be every woman's dream. The ideal man. His qualities are astounding. He's set the bar right up there. I have known men like Mr Rashidi, and of course, I've had the good sense of not marrying any of them. Wish you did the same. But that horse has already bolted, drool and all. Selma, I'll refer you to the psychologist Ernst Barogae. He said that males are like indoor plants. Plants whose water and sunshine content is in your hands. He may think he's in charge, but you need to slowly slip the rug out from under his feet. Stop catering to his basic needs. His food, clothes, physical needs. Just ignore him a lot more. He will then demand more, and throw tantrums. But this is a temporary phase. After a while if you continue to hold out, he'll start toeing your line, or better, go back to live with his mom.

Please try and get rid of this maid who could be his crutch, in this time of need. Cut off the supply of water and sunshine, and your plant will have to come around.

However, since there is no cure for the drooling, I would allow him to still walk a little ahead in public, so let's focus on him answering to you.

>Yours bestily,
>Cyrus

♥

This is Sanu George this side. I'm a medical student in a college in Thiruvananthapuram. In my class of eighty students, fifty-nine are boys and twenty are girls and one is yet to make-up his/her mind. I come from a very reserved family, and have never interacted with girls. I'm desperate to interact with them but just don't have the courage. Of the twenty girls, I find sixteen very attractive. But the other four I would not be able to entertain under any circumstances. I've tried a homeopathy course to boost my courage, but the positive results will take over two months to show. The homeopathy worked very well for my liver, and it has allowed me to go on drinking in peace. So I'm expecting good results with the courage pills too. Only problem is the time factor. You see the fifty-nine boys are like vultures. They all have the same plan as me. Several of them are on homeopathy too.

Serious competition! I need advice to scare off 2.6 boys at least, so I have a good chance of getting a girlfriend. Please help, I can't afford to wait.

Firstly I'm so glad that you are taking advantage of your medical surroundings, to the maximum. I, too, am a big fan of homeopathy. I find them very effective and they work better than mints. And I'm sure once the 'courage' pills kick in, you will turn into a 'ravager' of the ladies. A modern day Errol Flynn, Rajesh Khanna, Don Juan or Julio Iglesias, take your pick. However, you are rightfully super-concerned about the competition. More so, because they seem to be on the same pills as you, and as Flannagan's law of equality states, 'If all things be equal, love is very hard to be evenly distributed.'

Yours is per se, at least on the face of it, a mathematical conundrum. Fifty-nine per cent of you, trying to hold on to 16 per cent of them. These are strong odds, but if you move fast you can enter the front of the line. Now, while you have plumped for courage pills, I wish you had tried to take another popular homeopathy course—the

23½ Ways to Make a Girl Fall For You

you don't try to copy him, instead go for these three tried and tested methods.

(a) Zero in on not more than three potential female candidates. We need you to be focused. Can't go ahead and spray everywhere; (b) Start a casual conversation about nothing in particular, and see if you get a response. Topics could range from the role of earthworms in our ecosystem, to mundane occurrences in class, to favourite cuisine or art. I find less explored topics like 'How many provinces in China have 24x7 electricity,' to be very helpful. Simply because, if a woman finds a mundane topic with you interesting, than by process of elimination, it is you who is interesting to her, obviously not so much the topic; (c) Encourage a casual visit to the canteen. A sort of 'semi' date. Include others in this, but not any males vying for the same contender. To ensure this, you need to form weak alliances with a few males. So that everyone is clearly trying to put the basketball in different hoops. Remember the ancient Chinese saying, quoted 700 years before the invention of basketball, 'two basketballs can't fit in the same hoop, at the same time'.

If the girl responds, then by the time your homeopathy sets in, you'll be ruling the roost, so to speak.

My name is Andrew D'Souza. But because I look nothing like him, my friends call me Rooney—Rooney, as in Wayne Rooney, of Manchester United and England fame. I hate Manchester United. They are in my list of the five worst things in the world. The other four are Chelsea, Manchester City, Arsenal and cricket. You might be wondering why I hate Arsenal more than the sport of cricket. The answer is, I don't. I hate both of them equally. Now that I've shared my list of hates, let me share with you my list of loves. I love Liverpool Football Club and my Twitter handle was 'Steven Gerrard', right until the point when I was served a legal notice by representatives of the original Steven Gerrard. I have mounted and saved the legal notice and have hung it in my office. It's my dream come true. Actual correspondence from the original Steven Gerrard, to me! Even though, it was actually his representatives and the original Steven Gerrard doesn't know I exist! I mean I tried calling them but I couldn't understand their accents. And they obviously couldn't understand mine. As they kept putting the phone down on me. When the notice came, it was the happiest day when she moved one of my seven Liverpool pennants from its position, I should have sensed something was brewing. The thing is she just doesn't get football! And she had the temerity to ask me to remove my five foot poster of Gerrard which hangs over my bed. She says when she's naked she feels as though Gerrard is staring at her. She should be so lucky! As you know E.P.L matches are shown in the night for us in India because of the time difference. She's is now trying to stop me from watching football on TV. She has moved the TV out of our bedroom, and I fear I may be next. Please help.

Andrew D' Souza

I can't believe your letter. Really, what courage! I can't believe you still support Liverpool. They're gone 3000 years without any silverware. If you are going to topple your marriage, at least choose a worthy team, like Manchester City. Women versus football is an old tussle. An epic one. Along the lines of dogs and cats, Palestine and Israel, Ram Gopal Verma and Karan Johar. Of these only the Palestine–Israel tussle may one day be resolved.

If Liverpool is so important to you, how can Raell

(a) Get rid of Raell,
(b) Do a Liverpool and get rid of Gerrard,
(c) Get her to like football, or
(d) Start showing interest in her passions and hobbies.

Let's say first two are improbable. The first will cost you financially. The second will cost you emotionally. The third is a paradox and has never happened in the history of the world. That brings us to the final option. You need to start doing 'her' thing in order to continue doing your thing. Her 'thing' may be calisthenics, it may be bonsai plants, it may be renaissance art, or God forbid it may be the 'Art of Living'. Whatever, it is, don't think twice, dive in, and show interest.

This will need a hell of a lot of will power (and plenty of acting). You see, no self-respecting man can actually hold a conversation with a bonsai plant, or stare at any art which has no shred of nudity for more than three seconds! But, act you must. Your love for football must transcend your hatred for plants! A picture of Steven Gerrard with a bonsai plant super-imposed on a football at his feet may do the trick. I don't know too much about the 'Art of Living'. But, I'm told that it involves a lot of breathing.

23½ Ways to Make a Girl Fall For You

♥

Hi, I'm Madhukar from Mumbai. I am a Chemical Engineer and an MBA, and now I am working in a senior position in a leading bank. I specialize in house loans, and would love to have you avail of our facilities. And since you are a friend, I could get you a big dip in the premium that you'd need to pay.

My problem is that I'm falling for a colleague called Sneha. She's very pretty with long hair (natural), a super chest and hips (natural) and the smile of an angel (braces enhanced). She works in the backroom and I noticed her noticing me noticing her. So, after this happened a couple of times, actually forty-seven times in over three months. I finally gathered the courage to ask her out on a date, and we went for coffee in a nearby café. That's when my problem occurred, you see Sneha with all her beauty only speaks in Hindi. She is awfully unsure about her English. She, in fact, uses only three English phrases; 'Thank you'—which she uses instead of 'hello' and 'goodbye'; 'Goodbye'—which she wrongly uses instead of a person whose first language is Hindi. Please advise, as communicating with our eyes alone has its limits.

Now if you're looking for a four bedroom flat with attached toilets, as I know you have a big family, I know of a new building in central Mumbai, where we can help avail you of a discount as well as great deals, and that too on your preferred mode of payment. Please write back with your thoughts, as I think we can mutually benefit one another in the long run. Please also pass my enclosed phone number and email to your more affluent friends and contacts, as soon as possible.

Thanking you,
Madhukar

I'm seriously worried. I think you are just trying to hustle me. I get this feeling that your love problem is a ruse to snare me into your loan net. If that's the case then I must admit it's working wonderfully. Well, almost. As I'm more inclined towards a 3BHK with all facilities. Payment option? The more schemes, the merrier. And if you can get me a good personal discount from the builder, then I am very much interested in booking a flat, with the but let me assure you that not understanding each other can work out perfectly well for a couple.

Just take the example of the Stone Age man. Communication between a Stone Age man, and, often a stoned Stone Age woman, was kept to a bare minimum. The couple would point at important things, like body parts, food groups, and intruders, and immediately decide on a mutual course of action. Namely intercourse, eating and killing. Keep in mind this worked very well then! Minimum communication meant those ancient people had never even heard of divorce. That concept, came much after the Stone

Madhukar, couples who stay together communicate a lot initially. But as the years drag on, those who communicate less, last longer. Look around at older couples, and you will find this to be true. In fact, if interactions were kept to minimum, we'd have no need for diseases like Alzheimer's, and others that affect the senses and the memory.

Get off the shame block and go for it. Now about the housing loan, I'm sending you an email right now, and luckily for you, I'm sticking with English.

Yours hopefully,
Cyrus

I'm seventeen and in a confusing state right now. I want a girlfriend because I've always been single. But I don't get the right girl. And if I do manage to get a girl, I get her too fast and she runs away from me. This has led me into serious problems with other friends. Please help.
                                                                Kaurhik Ray

It's a simple case of a Twenty/Twenty player struggling to come to terms with test cricket. You are bloody quick at getting girls, right? However, they immediately run away. If I didn't know better, I'd say that this sounds like kidnapping. Kaurhik, don't rush in, and wait for a girl to come along who is special, whose very name, when you hear it, makes your heart race. Errm... not in the way Mayawati's name does, but in a happy, heightened, emotional way.

That's what I did. Unfortunately that girl got away, and now I'm married. So follow the four Ws: Wait, Watch, Woo and above all, don't forget to Wash.

                                                                Yours faithfully,
                                                                Cyrus

just been on my first date recently. It was a girl. I chose her because she was chubby, and I thought she wouldn't turn me down. She did though the first three times. I think she was hesitant to go out with me then, because I'm chubby too.

The date was for an English movie, starring George Clooney. He is her favourite actor. In the film, you may not, believe but he was chubby too. In fact, I swear to you, we watched the movie in a multiplex and out of a total of fourteen people in the audience, thirteen were… umm… a little chubby! And the only exception was just six months old and feeding, so it wasn't very safe for me to get a good look!

My worry is, do you think I can take the relationship to the next level? What if she thinks I chose her because she was chubby? I don't want her to think I asked her out because she was chubby, even though that's exactly why I asked her out. Also there was this incident, when we went to buy popcorn. We both hesitated to buy the butter version. Was that because we both independently wondered whether the other one would think of us as doing nothing about being chubby, and hence declined the butter popcorn and instead opted for a boring regular popcorn?

am I writing this to you because I feel more comfortable confiding in a chubby person? Oh, and what popcorn would you have bought, if you were in the same set of circumstances? And is your wife chubby? What about your previous girlfriends? Do you think I am in love with this girl? If so, is it because she's chubby?

Yours sincerely,
Devarshi

You have sent me more questions here, than have ever been sent in the history of letter writing. Not since 'semi erectus man' asked 'almost erectus man' for directions to the nearest hospitable care, have so many queries surfaced

Now, the main question here is, do you love this lady? And does she love you? The answer to this question, after much perusal and thought (during which I myself consumed seven tubs of butter popcorn, as well as one packet of caramel + cheese popcorn) is an emphatic NO!

You don't love her and she, in probability, doesn't even like you. After all, you asked her out based on a negative strategy, you made sure she paid for the date. During the avoid payment, this responsibility shouldn't have been yours in the first place. Devarshi, you don't love her and she, if she has any sense, should push your head into an icy bucket of cold water.

Let me share with you rule no.147 for dating a girl for the first time. Rule no.147 clearly states, 'When dating a girl for the first time, in order to have any success at all, at least pretend to like her.' Men forget that practice is a very important tool in successful dating. Success without some pretence is both unlikely as well as a tad pretentious. If you can't pretend sincerely, you can't love, it's as simple

Now let me tell you the good news, that I find you are actually capable of loving. So, there is hope for you. Yes, you are capable of loving, and I'll tell you that the identity of your love is crystal clear. It is butter popcorn! That's the one that you want. The one you've been waiting for. Now I refuse to answer questions on my wife, who in my eyes is forever young and beautiful. (Refer to rule no.147 for further explanation.) Devarshi, you are not ready for dating. For now, just stick to the butter popcorn.

Cyrus

allow you to know that a first date has been successful? Which brings me to the obvious second question. How does one know for sure that it's safe to ask for the second date? In fact, could you enlist all the rules and regulations that go with getting to a second date? I have been on nine dates this year, and couldn't get a second one for love or money. No literally, neither for love nor money. I couldn't get any of the nine girls to go out with me again. After the first two flatly said no, I just lost all confidence. So with the other seven, I just gave up after the first date. Let me put it this way, I'm still confident about the first dates. I'm not scared to ask women out. It's just that between the first and the second dates, I seem to lose my way. If it helps you, here are my details.

Name: Kishen Warsi

Weight: 59 kilos

Currently studying in the eight standard. Please note all my first dates were with grown women. To give you an example, Rita was thirty-seven, and on our date, she came to watch over me, while my parents were away at a function at night. In case of Prapti, who was twenty-

and talked. Of course, after the interval, a peculiar thing happened and she changed her seat. But for that one hour, I was in heaven. Can't even remember which movie it was, because of all the fun I had with Prapti. The one thing I have learnt so far, is that women are not so obvious with their feelings.

Yours sincerely,
Kishen

I don't know how to tell you this without hurting your feelings. The instances you mentioned don't qualify as dates. They qualify as any of the following—harassment, intrusive behavior, violating a person's privacy in a public place, dangerous encounter, a joke, or a non-date. Take your pick, and please don't cry.

A date is when you ask someone out, and she on her own accord agrees to go out with you. In some cultures men use charm to do this, in some they bribe the girl with cattle sheep and goats as ways of payment. But in all instances a date is only active or activated, when a girl agrees to go out with you by choice. Next, under the United Nations Trade and Regulations Act, 1957, an candidate for a thirty-seven-year-old. Frankly I must draw the line at twenty-two. If it's any consolation, I'll give you my own example. When I was 13½ years old, way back in 1985, I was madly in love with a thirty-six-year-old woman, my parents didn't approve of. But no one took the relationship seriously, primarily because of the difference in age, but also because Marilyn Monroe was already dead. So please stick to an appropriate age group as and when you do decide to go on an actual date. However, you are young and will have to, in all probability, go on a second date at some point. So let me anyway jot down the rules that govern the art of the second date. To go on a second date, you need to first have a decent first one. This first date can be categorized as decent if the girl hadn't: (a) run away in the middle of the date, (b) hit you with her hand bag, (c) cried and called her mother in the middle, (d) hit you with her high heel shoes, (e) pretended to faint just to end the date, (f) hit you with her platforms, (g) left with another man, and (h) hit you with the other man. If none of the above has happened, maybe there is potential in the first date converting into a second one. Before you do, check out these important clues: (a) Did she smile more than once at you during look back at you after saying bye? And when she looked at you was she digging her nose? And did you drop her home in the first place? And were you digging your nose at the time? (d) During the date did her foot accidentally rub against yours? And if so, did you respond without stamping on her feet?

These are all good questions, but the most important and simple cue of a decent date is, your date not falling asleep during the length and breadth of the date.

Keep in mind that the cues can also be complicated. If she says 'call me', she may mean 'don't ever call me'. She may even mean 'call me', when she says 'call me'. However, a 'call me', is better than an 'email me'. An 'email me' means, whatever you do don't call me. Yet, an 'email me' is better than an 'SMS me'. An 'SMS me' means 'don't call me, and don't bother emailing me'. But the worst possible news is if she says 'I'll call you'. This takes all the power of the date, wholly and solely, and puts it on her lap. 'I'll call you' generally means she's gone forever. Although it could mean 'I won't call you, you call me'. And on very rare occasions, it could also mean 'I'll call you', when she says 'I'll call you'. Of course 'I'll call you' is way better than 'I'll email you'. Which basically means other in public in the future.'

The end of your first date, probably gives you about a 70 per cent guarantee of whether you may have a second date. And of course, on that rare occasion, if the girl goes home with you, well then buddy, you are already on your second date. Well done! But that brings me to the third date. The third date? Well that's a story for another day.

Young man, when they tell you to reach for the stars, it doesn't mean you chase thirty-seven year olds. That would only make sense when you yourself are seventy. All the best. Slow and steady. If it works for tortoises, it

Cyrus

♥

I'm sorry to trouble you but I have a unique situation which is causing me deep distress. And it's all to do with canines. Of course, by canines I don't mean the teeth, I mean the species called dogs. And by dogs, I don't mean the analogical yet colloquial term for men who cheat on women, but actual dogs, the ones that operate on four

23½ Ways to Make a Girl Fall For You

Candy, because we were told she was a female by the breeder. However, we soon found out that in dogs, a large appendage around the under belly means that the dog could be male. We changed his name to Chaos. But since the servants insisted on pronouncing it as Chaos with a 'ch' as in church, we went back to Candy. I walk Candy in a park in Chennai, where a few weeks ago I met a pretty girl called Jahnavi, who walked a young dog called Lucky, a Cocker Spaniel. Lucky in all probability is male, but is too hairy for me to personally confirm that for sure. Jahnavi and I hit it off, but Candy would keep growling at Lucky. After a couple of weeks, the growling stopped. They started getting along, and so did we. Jahnavi and I went out on a couple of dates, things were going great until yesterday. Yesterday, I was in the park, and was about to propose to her when I realized Candy was chewing on Lucky as if he was a toy. I stopped Candy, but he had already chewed up half a ear of Lucky. It wasn't very serious, a few stitches, and Lucky should be fine. But not surprisingly Jahnavi started crying, and that's when it happened. In trying to be really sensitive about the incident, I said, and I quote myself, 'Hey Jahnavi, guess what? Lucky's name seems pretty ironic right now.' I has ignored all my apologies on text and phone. I really like her and feel really awful. Candy is sorry too! Please I hear you are a dog guy, how do I win Jahnavi back?

Vijay Murali

Let me tell you, as a professional dog walker (I have won several dog walking competitions) that dogs and our egos are inseparable. They are a like an Indian male and his paunch. Janhavi's ego is almost as upset as her sensibilities. Your attempt at humour was far worse than your Rottweiler's bite as well as your decision to name a ferocious dog, Candy. Judgment doesn't seem to be your

Here's what I suggest. Shoot a small video of Candy in submissive and apologetic poses. Then shoot one of you doing the same, lace it with voiceovers of what appears to be Candy's voice, use a light-talking male voice as for God's sake his name is Candy. The voiceover should be filled with apologies and assurances. In the end, appear to bite Candy yourself, to show some sort of farcical retribution. Please stay on the back foot until Jahnavi's ego is appeased. And in future, in delicate situations like such, if you don't

23½ Ways to Make a Girl Fall For You

Dear Mr Broacha,

Hi, my name is Namit Alimchandani. I'm a fashion model. I am enclosing my pictures. The first one has me full frontal in a swimming costume. You can immediately tell from my abs that I model. The second one has me in beachwear. I'm told the white sarong accentuates my immaculate jawline. The third picture has me in a suit. But as you can see, I've left one button undone, to showcase my abs. You can google me to verify my credentials and also check out my website, *GreekGodfromAmbala.com*. I have won 'Model of the year' in the Ambala gazette for the years 2007, 2008 and twice in 2009. I am an also in talks with various leading film directors for roles, over the past four years. Expect my debut film to happen anytime soon. My problem is concerned with my modeling. See, I have a perfect body and that has made me lose patience with people who don't have the same. In the past six months, I've been on dates with three different women. Let me share my anxiety over each one of them with you.

Shobha is in the cooperate line. She met me at a show, and was captivated by my abs. She came backstage and asked me to show them to her. I did, twice. So obviously

I cried all night. Why did she hide her fat from me? How could she have been so deceptive? After that you should think, I would have learned my lesson. But no! I bumped straight into Sudha. Sudha was a gym instructor, at the gym, where I work out. One day I was showing her my abs, and that's when I realized she was obviously interested in me. We also dated for a while, and then when the relationship got physical, got duped again. Layers of subcutaneous fat was clearly living around her thighs. In fact, her two thighs were joined together like one giant thigh. When she walked, I distinctly heard a 'whoosh' sound caused by one thigh coming in the way of the other thigh. At the gym, I had never noticed this before. I was stunned! How can the same thing happen to me twice in a row? I mean, I showed her my abs right at the beginning. So why couldn't she show me her thighs? I immediately broke up with this liar. For me she had violated the sanctity of our gym.

For a few months I avoided all women. Then I finally took advice from a senior male model. He had worked with Milind Soman, and had studied as high as the eleventh standard, so everybody went to him for advice. He told me to date from our fraternity. Not Ambala, but any hot

23½ Ways to Make a Girl Fall For You

Week extravaganza, when I was changing in the green room, that I noticed her looking at my abs. It was love at first sight. For her. She seemed to be in shape, so I accepted her proposal of asking me to ask her to go out on a date. Things went well, until at a recent modelling contest I saw her in the swimsuit round. And the bikini exposed her back fat. Yes, a layer of subcutaneous fat on her back, formed two small balloons under her bikini line. Not just me, but the judges also nearly threw up. Again, I was freaked out about the deceit. Why hide the back fat? I mean sooner or later I would have seen it. I even had her swear an oath, before dating, that she still practices Bulimia, on all Tuesdays, Thursdays and Saturdays. You know, vomiting right after all meals? And in spite of that, back fat? Was she lying? I dropped her like any sensible man would do, even before she could change out of that bikini. Her back fat still gives me right manes? But how can this keep happening to me? Why do all women hide their fat? Is it two much to demand a fat-free woman? I mean I'm very clear about my abs, so why can't they do the same? I'm now very upset with the duplicity and don't know if I'll ever date again. Please, can you guide

I hear your suffering. And no, it is not too much to ask. I like your refreshing honesty. Today, too many people pay lip service to other non-tangible, non-certifiable products, like personality, or sense of humour, or my biggest bug bear—sensitivity. You, on the other hand, are so awfully candid about your body beautiful, that you make all of us sound like hypocrites and fraudsters. At least, you are very clearly defined by two most noble thoughts: (1) A woman must have a terrific body (And by that you mean she should have no subcutaneous fat between heels and eyebrows). (2) They must like your abs. Ironically it's not that you have defined abs. But it's clearly the abs that define you. And why not? I have no advice for you, because you are actually completely sorted in your mind. You will not stand for less than a perfect form. However, this means that once you find that perfect girl, after a decade or so, you may need to let her go, and marry again. As the years will end, so will the perfection. So you constantly have to upgrade to a younger, updated model, loaded with all the features that must meet your requirements.

Of course, this depends on the quality of your abs, as the years go by. But going by your pictures, those abs seemed to be made of stone, so yes please don't settle for chins and necks to operate as one. In future watch out for that area too!

> Yours sincerely,
> Cyrus Broacha

♥

I read your column every Monday. These days we hear more breakup stories than love stories. I want to know if approaching a person that we love or maintaining a relationship is tough nowadays.

> Yours truly,
> Confused Geek

Dear Confused Geek,

Mr Geek, Shakespeare once said 'There is nothing either good or bad, but thinking makes it so.' Bear in mind, he's the same guy who also said '₹51 rupees for a litre of diesel? I'd rather walk!' My point is that whether the art of loving is tough or easy, it's actually up to you. My other main point is diesel has become costly, so please consider walking in future. Seriously.

I'm twenty-seven years old and a virgin. The problem is I think about sex all the time. This has been happening since I was fourteen. Okay, maybe not all the time. Sometimes I think about cricket too, but quickly my mind switches back to sex. For a while, I tried to do my own research and found out that wild animals, if they were not mated, would tend to get wilder. This explains why my cat Tubby bit me recently. As far as I know, Tubby has never been mated. And both him and I are getting more and more aggressive. Yesterday, I kicked a plant that was in my way, on the street. Then I screamed at a beggar for being so lazy at a traffic signal. I've also stared putting my phone down before saying a formal goodbye. And on many occasions, when the doorbell rings, neither me nor Tubby answer it.

What I want to ask you is guidance in having a sexual relationship. Since you apparently have two children, you must be having a vast knowledge on this matter. Also the obvious sub-question would be, how do I find a co-participant for this purpose, who is both willing and able? Also, I just want to have sexual relations the one time and that's it. I don't want any long term commitment.

have all day, and I take it for someone of your stature, these are standard questions.

Yours sincerely,
Sadanand

Can you also please help me find someone for Tubby. While writing this letter to you, I inordinately stepped on his tail, and he bit me again! That's the third times this

Dear Sadanand,

Firstly, I'm so glad you think I am an expert on the subject, because I can assure you nobody else thinks so, least of all my wife. Now, let's get on with your problem. You say that your bad temper and mood swings are because you haven't been mated ever before. And you base your deductions on studies of the love life of wild animals such as the American Bison, the Ridley Turtle, and the Mighty Komodo Dragon. All of those male members (excuse the pun!) wreak havoc on their environment, if they haven't been mated. Sorry to burst your bubble, Sadanand, but this theory is only partly true. Yes humans also get testy, but they don't always go berserk. For example William wreaked havoc, again, every single day of their lives, as well.

Your bad moods could be because of the delayed onset of puberty, Mumbai's rainfall, or even terrible heat rashes. What I mean is they can't be blamed on your lack of

Now to answer your second question. The answer would be the internet, i.e., social networking sites. For hook-ups, this is generally the best place to advertise. You can meet all sorts like-minded types. So Tubby should be able to find a mate in less than seven days. And in Tubby's case, once the act of coitus is done, he need not continue with the relationship.

You can also try your luck in finding a like-minded lady, interested in a one-off sparing session. Bear in mind that in 91 per cent of all cases, both partners are happy not to indulge in a repeat bout, even amongst humans. So you might get lucky, after getting lucky, either way. Sadly, I don't run a business where I could supply you with the needful. Though not to any lack of effort. But apparently such a business is frowned upon by our society, not to mention, its apparently illegal as well, but why don't you research the matter. You seem to do a lot of good spadework, may be you'll find that such a business

23½ Ways to Make a Girl Fall For You

♥

My name is Emanuel D'Costa. I'm in my twenties and I need your help. Especially, since I googled you and found out your dad is a lawyer. So, to be honest, I need his help. However, I thought if I asked you for help, you would then be able to get me his help, without me actually asking him for help directly. So that way I would get his help, but would have only requested your help! I think that's enough. Now here is my problem. I love this girl who lives in the next lane. I've loved her for the last seventeen years, six months and twenty-three days. Yet, I finally only told her about my love for her about three months ago. Can you guess what the result was? You can? You can't? Well, since I can't tell for sure, let me guess away for you. You can't. Fair enough, I'll tell you. Her name is Rebbeca, she is two years older than me, with a peach and cream complexion, and a face exactly like the actress Glenn Close. And when I first met her waiting in our neighbourhood as a young boy, I greeted her with a 'good morning'. She laughed at me. Firstly, because I though my heart was pinning and paining. I kept up our relationship. Always greeting her in the neighbourhood, sometimes with both hands, in an effort to pile on the pressure. We continued this song and dance even though her boyfriend was present, I would wait for her to come out of her building, no matter what time of the day it was (and on few occasions it was beyond midnight). I would nonchalantly greet her, and though she had genuine fear in her eyes, she would mumble something back. Finally, three months ago, I came to know that she had broken off with her last boyfriend. So seeing an opportunity I decided to dribble the ball into the goal. I waited for her one Monday morning, outside her building. As she took long to come out, I went behind the hedge in the building gardens, as I had to relieve myself. In the middle of the act, I heard her outraged voice say, 'What are you doing?' Dr Cyrus, I panicked and the only sentence that came out to my head was, 'I love you'. And that's when my problem started. You see, she had a court order put out on me, which said I'm never to be within fifty yards vicinity of her. That's where your father can come in to the picture. And for your part, how can I then take my relationship with Rebbeca to the next level?

them were really nasty, but never a doctor. While it's true I do have quite a plethora of college degrees, all completely bought and paid for with receipts, I must admit that I am not a qualified medical professional. Although, I could help you with stiffness in the shoulder and basic lower back pain, if push comes to shove (please pardon the pun). Having read your letter carefully, my father and I are both in agreement that you're extremely lucky that it's just a restraining order you have got from the court. Going only by your version of events, and without even considering her side of it, may I say that you deserve a far stiffer punishment (like banishment from the kingdom or being locked in a dungeon or even worse forced to wear Spandex only for the rest of your life). You, my friend, are the encyclopaedia description for the world 'stalker'. In the encyclopaedia in front of me, the world 'stalker' is defined as 'someone who stalks', which is clearly the work of an ill-read idiot. It should be changed to 'Emanuel D'Costa' with great speed and finality. You have stalked her for seventeen years, morning, noon, and night. You have scared the absolute Mickey out of her. Please understand, you can't force love. If we could, we'd all be married to Cindy Crawford. Both my father and I. And no, that seventeen years, six months and twenty-three days of your life surprising her at all times with forced greetings. If you spend seventeen years just saying hello to someone, and the conversation doesn't go any further, then that person must be a watchman! So, please, please stop with the wild stalking, and change your game.

Cyrus

Dad says Hi, and his consultation fee is ₹10,000 per day. Believe me, it's a steal. Also, was it you last evening behind my building compound wall? I distinctly heard the sound of someone relieving himself. Also, I have great connections with pharmacies, for any, shall we say, difficult-to-obtain medication.

♥

Well, dear reader, firstly I think we know each other well enough by now for me to dispense with this 'dear' nonsense. Let me just call you 'Reader'. Or even better 'Read'. Well, Read, I hope you realize how painstaking my work really is. And mind you, I do all this with no attempt to lobby for a Padma Vibhushan. Of course, the Padma Bhushan is another matter. Now back to the task at hand.

♥

once invented a mythical creature called the 'Gambozo' in my dream. To describe the Gambozo to you would take me days. But in short, he was a large terrestrial beast, about sixty feet long and fourteen feet tall with one round of cylindrical wing, and a scaly coat! He had short front paws and powerful hinds, and was carnivorous by nature. However, on Thursdays, he only ate grasshoppers. And although he had no known predator to fear, he himself had a horrific terror of trees.

So, you can see what a magical mind I have. It truly is magical. Once in my mind, I was on *MasterChef Australia*, and cooked a dish that never existed before called 'Orange Mulcatti'. Obviously, I won the competition and was so popular that I soon replaced Matt Preston as a judge on the programme. Then went on to become the Premier of New South Wales, and in time founded a brand new island colony close to Tasmania! With such an avid array of thoughts, I find it difficult to keep friends. As I find, many friends just can't keep up with me. They are just too mundane and boring. Furthermore, since their minds haven't developed as much as mine has, I tend to look down upon them, and scoff at them. This has seriously dented my chances with the ladies. And that's probably have any friends at all, but basically I have a negative amount of friends. I'm in the red zone basically when it comes to friends. The other day, even the shopkeeper closed the shop on me. It was 11.30 in the morning and he had four customers inside at the time. He basically locked them in just so that he could keep me out! How am I ever going to meet girls now? I often wonder if it was this bad socially for other similarly advanced minds like J.K. Rowling, Woody Allen, and Enid Blyton, and the guy who writes *Dr Who*?

Can you please tell me if these guys also didn't get invited to parties? And if so, how did they get dates? Please don't make me pay for my brilliance. It's a real shame, if I can't share my beautiful mind with someone else.

Yours sincerely,
Manu

I am not really sure about your brilliant mind, but I have a problem with your brilliant letter. Here are a few of my observations: (a) You use 'basically' far too much in your writing, (b) the 'Gambozo' you described sounds exactly like the description of a Tyrannosaurus Rex with and (e) There is already a colony near Tasmania; last time I checked it was called New Zealand.

So, as far as I'm concerned Manu, you are no J.K. Rowling or Woody Allen or Enid Blyton. Although you are clearly better than the guy who writes *Dr Who*.

So let's dissolve this 'brilliant mind' theory out of the equation. In fact, I suggest that you pretend you didn't have a brilliant mind but instead had a simple, straight forward, not full of yourself, mind-cum-personality.

Using this new base, start meeting new people, especially girls. Follow the set of rules listed below while doing so

> Don't talk too much, in fact, don't talk at all. Try to listen instead.
> After listening to the other person, don't try to correct the person or the person's comments.
> There is no need to give marks to the person you are interacting with. For instance, if a girl you met, let's call her Amisha, says 'Hi, what's the time?' You mustn't answer with, 'You get only four out of ten marks for that question, since you have a watch on your arm and you shouldn't have asked

To get on with 'lesser' minds, please come down to their level. The ancient Peruvian tribe, the Zu Zaras, had a saying, 'Play fair, play hard, don't participate'. Even today in North Eastern Peru the punishment for pontification and self-glorification is death. I hope this clears your... er... brilliant mind.

Yours sincerely,
Cyrus

♥

I approached one of my school friends on Facebook. She used to chat with me till late nights. Now, after a month, I have started liking her. However, she has reduced chatting with me and that bothers me. I am unable to concentrate on my studies. She seems to like me, by the way she chats with me. Sometimes I call her 'baby' and she doesn't mind. In fact, she calls me 'baby' too. I don't understand what her feelings are for me. Is she testing me or could it be

Yours sincerely,
Anonymous Admirer

Sharma's marginal utility theory, this is normal. After the initial surplus, you come to a more balanced amount of time spent chatting, so don't panic as yet. Your second concern is the use of the word 'baby'. Normally, this term is used for a human child under ten years of age, who is not very fat, i.e., under sixty kgs. It's also a term of endearment used between adults of both sexes. This is a good sign. So prima facie, it appears 'baby' likes you 'baby'. Now please don't jump the gun and start having babies.

Yours sincerely,

Cyrus

♥

I'm Rupak, originally from Hampi, in the south. My father is a doctor (his actual designation is Andrologist). But, I never use that description because most people are unfamiliar with Andrology. And when I say Andrologist, they assume he was some sort of explorer or fossil hunter. Of course, having seen some of his patients, I do agree the word fossil is not entirely out of place. He has now got a great new job in Bangalore city. Sorry, Bengaluru city. This experienced girls. I mean I know what they look like, but I've never had a chance to meet them up close. In Hampi, girls are like crows. And by that I mean if you try to get near, they just somehow know, and fly away. So, I need some tips on how to deal with girls at close quarters. In this new American school in Bengaluru, there are sixteen girls and just fourteen boys. I'm going to see them up close everyday. My queries are these. What do you say to girls? Can you give me some good lines? Are you allowed to stare? If so, for how long? Once you are friendly with a girl, can you then treat her like a boy? And by that I mean can you slap her on the back? Pull her hair? Mess up her tie? Burst a brown paper bag on her head? Steal her lunch? And copy her notes? Please do answer specifically as Bengaluru is a big city, and also a very hip city. I do want to make a good impression. My aim is to have my first girlfriend before my sixteenth birthday.

Yours sincerely,
Rupak

You know what the great baseball legend Sammy Soza said, 'Before you make a century you first have to make take your queries one by one. First, you ask, what do you say to girls? Well, if you don't know them, best is to be polite and not make sounds around them. Say normal things like 'Hello', or 'Shall I move that chair?', or 'Shall I clear your path?' You say all this softly while maintaining eye contact, but not by staring intensely like you are the main character in a Rahul Bose film. You never say 'You are standing on my foot', even if they are. And never say our hair went in my eye', even if it did and temporarily blinded you. As for good lines, please avoid cheesy ones like 'My life started after I met you'. This is scientifically impossible and will fool only the sufficiently medicated ones. I prefer normal lines to be used initially, such as, 'This way', or 'It's too hot', and my personal favourite, 'I can't believe it's Hindi period next' (keep in mind the last one only works when it really is Hindi next or she'll see through your ruse). Other winner lines include, 'Look I can sign with my left hand'. 'Knots and Crosses?' And 'Hell, the teacher's come' (keep in mind it's better to yell 'The teacher's come' only when the teacher actually arrives or she'll see through your ruse). When it comes to staring, it varies from culture to culture. In China, 3.4 seconds is the norm. In Europe, it's 2.85 seconds, and in most applied then the seconds don't matter. In simple English, that means, if she's not facing you staring has no cut-off.

Now about treating her like a boy, please don't do that. Overfamiliarity doesn't work with most ladies. If girls needed to be treated like boys, why would they be girls in the first place? So please don't misuse the secularism. So no slapping, anything anywhere, ever. No touching her hair, so forget pulling. Girls generally don't wear ties, but if so, please don't pull it. The brown bag idea is a good one, only if you want to break up with her. And at age fifteen-and-a-half, stealing lunch of a boy or a girl will not be justified, even if you are severely underweight or of unsound mind, and mistook her samosa for yours. But you may, with her prior permission, copy her notes. Treating a girl like a boy can only work after twenty years of marriage, and that's only if both partners are confident of going at it for another twenty.

Mr Rupak, it's best to apply the different but same formula. Girls are different from boys, but like to be treated in the same way you treat yourself. With great love, greater respect and lots of toilet breaks. And when you meet the girl who reminds you of you, then you have the best chance of a content and long-lasting relationship. And then, you

23½ Ways to Make a Girl Fall For You

♥

This is Raayaan Masbuwala writing to you. Before I get to my problem, let me tell you a bit about myself. I work in a large family business. We take orders for pharmaceutical companies from pharmacies and then get them delivered. Obviously, if you ever want a drug and don't have a proper prescription, then you need to come to me. I'm twenty-seven years old. I have a good height to weight ratio. My body mass index (B.M.I.) is also average. I have no favourite colour. I don't enjoy vacations. I'm not a real foodie. I don't enjoy sports. I'm not comfortable at parties, and I don't believe in social networking. I've never understood the need for hobbies, and I'm allergic to pets. Also, I have no interest in cinema, absolutely can't relate to art and sculpture, am scared of the theatre, and terrified of the circus. Leave alone the Aquarium!

Ever since my first standard, I've been labelled 'boring'. While the label boring, doesn't bother me, it has affected my 'social life'. Although, I can say I'm crazy about girls (I have dated a couple of them). However, in all came back. When I asked her later about this incident, she finally broke down and confessed. Her rationale was that after meeting the pigeons for a few seconds, she just found them that little bit more exciting than me! Another girl, Zayee, did an even worse deed. When I went to fetch her from her home, for our second date, she did a peculiar thing. On seeing through the peep hole, she tried to escape from her second floor bathroom window, by scaling down the pipe. Halfway through this endeavour, she lost her foot and fell. As they carried her to an ambulance on a stretcher she made the doctor swear, he wouldn't give out her hospital's location to anyone. This just highlights the fact that everyone thinks I'm boring. The real problem is that now my parents want to get me married. They've given me a deadline of one year to find my own bride, or they take over. So the real question is, how do I get a girl, any girl, to fall in love with me?

Yours,
Raayaan Masbuwala

Your problem is best answered by the famous Roman thinker Cato. Unfortunately, Cato is dead so we don't know alongside him. Socrates's final words on earth were 'All I know is that I know nothing.' Whether this is true or not is contentious to prove today. As recent evidence found in Greece tell us he may have said, 'Ouch! My stomach!', a little after that. But whatever be the truth, there is compelling evidence, that he definitely, at the very least, said 'Ouch!' What can be proved beyond doubt is that his brother Procrates, in a rare display of brotherly love and solidarity (they hadn't talked for twenty seven years before that day, after an earlier incident where Socrates had worn Procrates's slippers after a common family public bath), replied to him, 'All I've done, is I've done nothing'. Six hours after his death, Socrates was buried with his slippers (the right ones this time). Eight hours later, he was fully forgotten by the Grecian Society, aside for a handful of cobblers. It was Procrates who became Athens's new swinging sensation. And his call to do nothing, glamourized the concept of immobility. And soon those who did very little became the ancient world's version of 'Rock Stars'. Obviously the woman followed. A fact borne out by Procrates, dying of syphilis, eight months later.

Raayaan, the point of the story is that was then. This is now. Today, Socrates is remembered. And barring myself an alligator can't fast on Fridays. But you can pretend to like things, while being honest only with yourself. Pretend to show interest. This pretence could stand you in good stead. It'll help you climb quickly up the social ladder. And it might help you cope with the biggest pretence of all. The one in which two people spend over forty years together in the same house with children, and sometimes grandchildren too.

Yours less lovingly,
Cyrus

♥

Recently I went on a cruise ship. It was called *La Marina*, and was like a five-star hotel on the sea. I went along with five of my friends. All of us were male. Out of the five, three are divorced. And one doesn't like girls, if you know what I mean. So I guess I was the only 'hunter' in the party. On the first day, we found a group of girls. We all hit it off. They were also a group of five, and that's where the problem happened. I liked this girl Anita. She's a national level gymnast. She won the gold medal in the who went to the bar. And hurt his head. Bar, get it? Steel bar? Anyway, she loved all my bar jokes, and I though she liked me as much as I liked her. We ate together and hung out together. However, on the last night, we all went dancing, and when the slow numbers started Anita walked off. Before I could ask her to come back, another girl, Pisha, asked me to dance with her. Since it was a slow number, I had to hold her hips. While dancing I kept looking over Pisha, trying to locate Anita. While doing so I toppled over Pisha, and we both fell on the ground. Since Anita saw the commotion and looked right at me, I had this soft look in my eyes. Pisha though it was for her. Bottom line: when we all returned to Mumbai, Anita did not respond to my calls, and instead Pisha is hounding me with SMSs. How can I rectify this situation? I don't know if Anita is upset or not interested. Please help me win over Anita, and if that's not possible, please help me get rid of Pisha forever. I really don't want to be seen out with her. People will start taking pity on me. So please help!

Yours sincerely,
Mr Mahtosh

think you have made a very gross mistake. Your mistake is you think women are exactly like TV channels. And you can put one off and simultaneously switch the other one on. But even in TV channels there is no guarantee that this will always happen. Especially, if like me you have a ATTA Sky connection. A little rain and you are forced to go back to primitive, medieval forms of entertainment. Like reading! Now I need to share a very vital piece of information with you, Mahtoshji.

This is about the famous sense of humour business. Throughout your life, you have probably read or heard this phrase that women like men with a sense of humour. Let me tell you this is a myth, a complete fabrication, a lie in progress. This idea that women like men with a sense of humour can be placed along the greatest lies of all time. You know like Tyrannosaurus Rex could do handstands, Kim Jong-un is Mother Teresa's first cousin, and Indians set the standard for civic consciousness and punctuality worldwide. If women love a sense of humour, then why did Oscar Wilde die a lonely old man in Paris? (Okay maybe that's not the right example.) Closer home, how many girls flocks to Johnny Lever, Raju Srivastav, and I dare say, myself. Compare the results with the amount laughed. But that still doesn't mean she likes you. In fact, I'm inclined to wager that if you and John Abraham took part in a contest for Anita, in which you cracked five jokes in one minute, and he simply sat on a chair for the same amount of time, doing nothing, he'd still win Anita's hand and in all probability the rest of her as well. The fact is she's avoiding your calls. So please follow the 'three phone step' as ordained by international law, i.e., if the girl fails to reply to three consecutive phone calls, then you need to accept that she's completely forgotten you.

That brings us to Pisha. First, what kind of name is Pisha? Very odd indeed. I've heard of Tisha, Lisha, Nisha, even Visha. But never a Pisha. In fact, she sounds like a bodily sound if you say her name aloud quickly. But don't worry, remember Chairman Mao's famous couplet. Not the one about killing millions to bring down the population, the other one. The one where he says if you are offered a chair, return the favour with a table of the same size. This may partly explain why tables in China are the same size as chairs. Although, why soup bowls are the same size as the chairs, remains a mystery? The couplet basically means, do unto others what another girl Anita did to you. That is, follow the same above mentioned 'three phone step'. If (electronics store) for after sales service. I'm hopeful to beat Charlie Sheen's record by early next week, by the way.

Mr Mahtosh, while we must make every endeavour to woo the ladies, and you must try every combination and permutation you can, please remember that we must know when it's checkmate, so that we can move on to the next one. I'll let you into a last secret. If you hound and scare a girl, by not giving up, and chasing her relentlessly, she then passes on news of your behaviour to others, thus squashing any future chance you may have with the rest of womanhood. All women have a direct hot line to one another. Unlike us, they have unionized many centuries ago. So forget about Anita, and patiently wait it out till Pisha (what a name) gives up on you. Let's not forget Sun Yat Sen's immortal words: 'A Pisha in hand is worth more than two Anitas in the bush.' If you know what I mean.

Yours helpfully,
Cyrus

♥

I'm very close to my best friend. The problem is I love her

turns bad. I want to know whether she's ready to get into a relationship with me without spoiling our friendship.

Yours sincerely,
Rushin Shah

Brother Rushin,

You already set a dynamic in place by having this best friend relationship with her. Sun Tzoo in his book *War Tales for Everyday Use* says: 'I'm changing battle formations, mud-battle leads to indigestion'. Please gauge how she feels about the other guy. If it's serious, back off for now. Or you'll get indigestion to go with your aching heart. Sooner or later you'll have to come clean. Time it well, so that you have a better chance of success. Strike when the iron-board is empty. Also Sun Tzoo used to run a laundry (I know 'cliché' but what can you do).

Yours sincerely,
Cyrus

♥

I don't think you would have ever received a letter like mine

My issue is that all women love me. I'm a veritable 'chick magnet'. And this is not a recent phenomenon. Let me tell you a story, going back to when I was a teenager. Every day, seven to eight girls would walk me from my house to the bus stop, a distance of eleven-and-a-half feet. Then while returning, they would once again reverse the process, and walk me from the bus stop to my doorstep. When I was just thirteen years old, the girl fan club varied from the ages of nine to sixteen! This situation didn't change geographically. When I used to visit Dehradun for summer camp vacations. I would get a lot of female attention there as well. Locals in fact would joke that all the tigresses were missing from the forest, because they were chasing me! In the U.S. it was just the same. I never had to do any homework, or housework, or stand in lines, or get food to my table, or drive a car. All this would be done for me by over-enthusiastic girls who would wait on me hand and foot. Unfortunately, all this love and attention has become too much. I feel suffocated, and I'm having anxiety attacks. I can't go to any public places if there are any ladies present. I won't venture into restaurants if they have female staff members. And yesterday, I broke a red light while driving and a female policewoman stopped her away. It doesn't end there either. Last night when I looked out of my window, I could see her motorbike doing rounds of my neighbourhood. It's a good ten kilometers off her regular beat. How the hell am I ever gonna find true love? Under all the fawning and following, I would never be able to identify love at all? I mean who am I? Elvis? Justin Bieber? The entire One Direction? Salman Khan? Ranveer Singh? Hrithik Roshan? Please help me find real love, with a real girl?

Yours dependently,
Faheem Merzia

You really have an interesting story. I can't decide whether you are the greatest man to have ever lived, or a really an unfortunate suffering soul. And whether you are Elvis, Justin Bieber, the entire One Direction, Salman Khan, Ranveer Singh or Hrithik Roshan? Well, the answer has to be, all of the above. Faheem, quite frankly I don't know why you are complaining? Stop being so sensitive. You've got the attention, love, and control of millions of women for the rest of your life. You are living every man's dream and every man's fantasy, barring Elton John. Embrace your dropped me to the bus stop today? My pop. You know who brought me home from my bus stop? My pot-bellied, paan chewing cook, Mandesh. And mind you, Mandesh looks like a little bus himself!

If we refer to Howitzer and Harish's Romantic Almanac, page 97 paragraph 3, it will clear your mind. It says, and I quote, 'If a man finds himself the object and desire of a plurality of women, on a daily basis, he must attempt to give back to society, as an appreciation of his great luck. He could join an N.G.O. and work with the nerdy, the destitute, and the suffering. He could also contribute financially, through donations, or building of schools, hospitals and or toilets. But give back he must, in an effort to gain A.K. (adjusted karma).' Faheem, you are this lucky man. You don't see it this way, much like a superstar may hate this super success. But you won't get much support and sympathy. As long as you co-exist in society, it seems like women will be drawn to you. Your best bet to find love then, is to do a thorough vetting process. Let me stress that's vet with 'v'. And it's not where you take your sick pet to either. Each and every girl, and I mean each and every one of them, you'll have to study to see if she's that 'special one'. Just like all the others, she too will be

23½ Ways to Make a Girl Fall For You

life around women who are crazy about you, but is that really so bad? To find your one diamond, I'm afraid you must go through the rough. Moreover, let me tell you my one uncle has rickets, a friend of mine has lost his job in the Gulf and is being sent back, another relative isn't sure if he is a man or a woman, and I, myself, have started urinating in three separate shifts. Those, Farheen, are real problems. Having girls chase you, however bad you feel, just can't be considered a problem. And if it is a problem, it's the best one to have. One more thing, consult an aroma therapist. You may be emitting some phenomena that is inducing the women towards you. This is even more of a possibility if females of all species cats, dogs, insects, gerbils et al. are also drawn to you. My friend Javed had a similar problem. Women and men and animals (but not insects) were drawn to him. However, his aroma therapist advised him to try something different, like bathing, which he hadn't done in years, and within days the problem was fixed. Not only that, even his wife and family left him. You'd never meet a more grateful man. Although now in public places he does get engulfed by insects. Hey, no one can win them all.

Yours sincerely,

Please help me. I needed your help yesterday. I wanted your help so badly that in my original letter I just wrote the world 'Help!' 271 times and was about to send it. Then it hit me, that I had spelt it wrong in fourteen of those instances. It also occurred to me that other than 257 'Helps' and fourteen 'Helpps', I wouldn't be sending you adequate information about my problem. In fact, I'm told that one word correspondences are only self-explanatory, if the word used is cancelled! Don't misunderstand me, the word itself shouldn't be cancelled. Rather, the word written in the document should be the word 'cancelled'. Clear? Okay, just to further throw light on my point, here is a list of words that I feel should be cancelled: (a) panty hose, (b) blunt, (c) tumble turn, (d) Gestapo, and (e) turmeric. The last one is only there because I'm allergic to it. You may have guessed by now that I am an educator. I was told by my twelve-year-old nephew Mikhaail, that I'm a 'brain feeder'. Please add this expression to that list. Well, I suppose that's what I am. I help young brains sprout. Although some are obviously 'unsproutable' (add to the list please). The subject I spread is the whole gamut of prefer deer to midwives. Some would just prefer deer to wives. But that is some other people's problem.) Let's go back to my problem. My problem is that although I'm thirty-four years of age, I'm unable to find and woo a member of the opposite sex long enough for her to marry me. I've had four relationships. One with Delna lasted for four months. Although three of those months she was in London doing a 'Cordon Bleau' course. And she promptly broke up with me at the airport where I went to pick her up on her return. With Avi, it lasted eleven days. Here again, she was sick with measles for most of the time, which would mathematically be roughly eleven days. With Pranali, it lasted two days and the last woman who agreed to go out with me, Eela, never turned up. As an educator, I have an analytical mind, so I've strung together all the main reasons I suspect for my unsuccessful, or rather, semi-successful love life. They are (a) I'm short, (b) I'm thirty-four, (c) I'm over-educated, and (d) I'm too nice. Maybe you could zero in on my so called inadequacy in love, and like I said at the start, 'Help me!' My name is Professor Samir Shrike, Thank you.

Dear Professor,

monsoon, and (e) technetronic. Professor, let me assure you that I took your letter very seriously. I read it eight times, and then I had my wife read it out to me, while performing her customary, compulsory, Surya Namaskar. After her reading, I was so dejected I felt like informing you that 271 consecutive 'Help!' words may have been far clearer. Then I did what I always do when I'm facing a perplexing problem. I ran away. When I returned home, I took a shower. It was in the shower, while singing and thereby choking under the force of an open shower tap, that I solved the riddle. I damn well threaded the needle. I crossed the Rubicon, I pulled the tooth of the tiger. You see your letter exposes your personality. It's not visible to the common gaze, but to my trained eye it stood out like an Indian in an ice-hockey rink. You talk too much. The reason why Delna, Pranali, Avi and Eela ran away as fast as they could is simple. You talk too much. And by doing so, you broke a sacred covenant. You breached the walls of Babylon. One of the oldest gender stereotypes still allowed around the globe, is that women like to talk. It's one of the few stereotypes which don't always cause offense. Women like to talk, Professor. You, curiously, love to talk too. And being an educator, and a 'brain feeder', you'll be

23½ Ways to Make a Girl Fall For You

Shirke, women get turned off because you are out-talking them. I don't blame you since it's your basic personality trait. And one should swerve off one's natural personality traits, unless you are a sociopath and that trait is murder. (Also please add 'sociopath' to my cancelled words list kindly.) My good educator, when you venture into the other gender's space you are heading for a collision, and that means damages. How would you like it if they took over our traits? You know like laziness, or bodily sounds, or grunting. Bear in mind, grunting is both a bodily sound, and a very effective tool of communication. Come on Professor Shirke, either learn to pull back (no pun please) in the company of the ladies, or find that rare White Whale. That rare Snow Leopard. That rare sighting of a pretty version of the Lochness Monster. And by that I obviously mean, a woman who rarely talks. Believe me, I'm told they are in short supply. And if not, they have a whole pantheon of suitors standing in line, so, hurry! But, on another note, please stay in touch. I loved your cancelled words game. Here are a few more. Bulbous, juggernaut, misappropriate... sexist...

Yours truly,
Cyrus

I name is Amanpreet and but my friends call me, the 'Smoothee'. That name happened because of my reputation. My friends say I'm real smooth with the ladies, so smooth that the ladies can't hear me coming. LOL! It appears that most girls can't say no to me. It's to do partially with my deep velvet voice, I think. But all this changed when I met Aparna. Aparna is considered the prettiest girl on the campus. I'll never forget the first moment I saw her. I was sipping on a huge ice-cream float (vanilla flavour) in my hand when she passed me by in the tightest of pants. Pants that were so skintight on her even air couldn't have passed through. I was absolutely mesmerized, so much so that I dropped my freezing cold, sticky wet, squishy ice-cream flat on Mandira, who was my girlfriend at the time. As she screamed in horror, I remember being very happy at the incident occurring as I knew it would be far easier to break up with Mandira now. And after being floored by Aparna, a break-up with Mandira was not just optional, it was compulsory! I don't even remember saying sorry to Mandira. As I write this I can't even remember what Mandira looks like. The only visual that flashes in also. Such is the power of this girl. Now, moving on, I used all my smothee powers and pataoed Aparna. It wasn't easy and took longer than my normal batting average of one week. Up until this point we've been on three dates, and we haven't done anything physical yet. Not because of her (in fact, at our last movie date she was trying to kiss me while person after person was getting murdered on screen), but because of me. The moment we actually spent time together I noticed something sinister. You know, how some people have putting off traits, such as running noses, gas emissions, or uncontrolled love for religion? Well Aparna has one of these. In fact hers is the worst one of all. She suffers from heavy breathing. She sounds like a Qawali artist warming up. Not only that, if you are close to her then her breath can hit you like a torrent of hot air. When I first experienced it, we were in my car, and I thought there was a storm approaching. And it was while checking weather conditions on my phone that I realized that I was dating Darth Vader. Actually I think I've gone too far with that comparison, because at least Darth Vader looked like he would breathe heavily like Darth Vader. Aparna looked like Aparna and what I got was Darth Vader. So, my apologies to the real Darth

Vader to turn to, I must turn to you. Please understand that I really like Aparna, she's one in a million. But I can't date a ship leaving the harbour! Make no mistake the sound effect is deafening, and the breadth hits you like a supercharged heater. How do I tell her? What could she do? How can I go to second base under such frightening

Dear Mr 'Smoothee',

As I reply to your pitiful predicament, let me tell you I totally identify with what you are feeling, which is fear. I'm writing this on a plane which is refusing to land. We are in a tremendous traffic jam. Last I heard we are scheduled to be the 589th plane to land. Which means at least three birthdays and one World Cup may happen inside this plane. The passenger next to me has suggested that I turn this whole reply into a sixteen part book, since we have the time. I thought that was a really a good idea, but unfortunately my answer to you will only take three or four sentences. What you are feeling is ambivalent love. You want her badly but are also repulsed by her. It's similar to what Christopher Columbus felt when he reached America. He was repulsed to go just anywhere as in keeping with local customs. A practice which is still prevalent in India as of today. My suggestions are be honest. Delicately tell her that the breathing is slightly excessive, but please don't try to train her. Nothing will chase a woman away faster than trying to change her to suit your needs. Well maybe loud Qawali singing, but nothing else really. Just as Columbus got used to people ignoring him, spend more time with Aparna and face her heavy breathing head on. First for a few minutes, then an hour, then in time, get used to it. As for what she can do about it, homeopathy, facing the other way, and wearing a mark spring to mind. But if you really want to reach second base, face the music. Errm… sorry the breathing! Learn to love her for who she is, and not who you need her to be. Christopher Columbus would have expected no less.

Yours faithfully,
Cyrus

A statutory general warning. Letter writing consumption should be restricted to a moderate level. The Surgeon General has determined that too many letters are bad for the nervous system. So keeping

I like a boy. I chat with him almost everyday. But lately he seems to be less interested in chatting with me. He almost ignores me and my chats. Initially, things were not like that. I used to get his attention and he was really interested in knowing about me, which isn't the case anymore. I gave him a break of six days so that he misses me and talks to me again. I am really obsessing over this guy. It's just that I am in love with him. What should I do, forget him anyway and move on or I still have my chances?

Akeera

There's a reason why animals mate seasonally. And it's not all to do with availability of hotel rooms. It seems like his love machine is running dry. He's less inclined. He's changed his mind. Mine is not there (sorry I got carried away!). Give it a break then pick up again. If he's still cold, there's not much you can do. After all you can take a horse to water but not if he insists on the mineral stuff.

Yours faithfully,
Cyrus

It's really a pseudonym. I've taken it after the artist Neil Sedaka who is my favourite. Most people though can't fathom how Hari Prasad Gujjar can become Sedaka. My own Chacha said, what's wrong with the boy, why take that name? It's not like he's got Japanese blood!

I'm an accomplished musician by the way. I can play the piano, guitar, bass guitar, and the tabla using alternate hands only. I also write my own songs and upload them on the internet. You may have downloaded some of them. Like 'Life is Like a Bone China' and 'This Cradle Ain't Getting No Wind', for more likes than dislikes. 'And Love is Worse than Diabetes', was a dead heat in likes and dislikes. Strangely what I consider my greatest work (you surely have heard of this one), 'Bhel Puri Chutney and Wine', was under-appreciated. I got a lot of negative reviews for it. One critic called it the worst human sound ever recorded after belching. Then he himself got a lot of flak from others, who felt belching was actually an improvement on 'Bhel Puri Chutney and Wine'. I even considered making that the title of my next song—'Belching is Better than Bhel Puri Chutney and Wine'—but then decided to wait for the controversy and criticism to die down, before slipping this new number in. Of course, I comfort myself in Carnatic vocals, which I can't bear. I see no logic to Carnatic vocals, starting with the spelling. If the state Karnataka is spelt with a K, why are its vocals spelt with C? Anyhow we started dating, and on all counts she's a lovely girl. But then a little while back, she forced me to attend a concert of hers. I thought I was going to collapse in the concert hall. At one point, it sounded like a person is being skinned alive while singing. And that was only the anchor introducing her act! Worse was to follow. Her Act! When they broke for interval, I started crying, and that was primarily because the anchor threatened us by saying that the second half was a lot longer. I tried to do the decent thing and lie to her after the concert. But when she started practicing the cacophony in the car, not to mention play her own audio recordings simultaneously, I broke down and confessed that I liked Carnatic vocals as much as a hole in my head. My exact words were, 'Isn't hearing animals make high pitch drowning sounds better than watching them drown on National Geographic?' She was totally enraged. In her ballistic reposte, she criticized 'Bhel Puri Chutney and Wine', and said it is the worst sound she was ever forced to hear. I tried to make her see reason, by suggesting that in that case, she should listen to or reacting. I actually can't handle Carnatic vocal stuff. Period. Please help if you can, Mr Cyrus?

Sedaka

Dear Mr Sedeka,

My name is Cyrus Broacha and not Broacha Cyrus. Unless of course, you are writing it in Persian, yet reading it in English. Let me start by saying I downloaded 'Bhel Puri Chutney and Wine', and I will say this, at least you looked nice. Music, like all art, and some politics, is very subjective. Homo marinus, one of our earlier primitive forefathers, found out they liked the sound of stone against stone. Which became the precursor to modern music. Neanderthal men who followed Homo marinus, evolved that music form into stone beating on Homo marinus's head. This produced a wonderful vibrant musical art form for its time, and also wiped out Homo marinus. So what Neanderthal men loved as music, Homo marinus didn't appreciate at all. Coming to Carnatic vocals, I totally get your point. I too can't seem to stomach it. I once tuned violently ill looking at a poster of it outside a popular theatre. Then I confronted myself with this thought, 'At least it's not Hindustani Classical!' Whatever you are feeling the next performance. Give her a nice present backstage. Convince her and yourself that you are developing an ear for Carnatic vocals. In actuality, use all your mental strength to tune out of the auditorium, house, or car, when this music is being played. Read this book by Sen and Sen

Teleporting the Mind. It shows you how to build the mental strength and flexibility to transport the mind away from a sinister place that the body is in. It's based on Victor Frankls lost early works on how he endured Auschwitz. In other words, in time she could be screaming away on stage like a couple of roller skates in heat, but you will be in exotic Kingston, Jamaica surrounded by a group of super hot girls and listening to old school reggae. If you don't convince her, you enjoy her talent. The relationship has lesser chances of surviving than Homo marinus did, as musical tastes and demands changed. The only other option is to actually go deaf. And like anyone who went to a Carnatic vocal concert and tried to tell the tale will tell you, 'It's a pretty sensible option, for sure'. All the best, and one more thing. Maybe it's best to keep her away from 'Bhel Puri Chutney and Wine', for a while. I'd go with, let's see… ummm… technical difficulties. Works wonders worldwide.

Five months a year in the Lakshswadeep Islands. The company I work for is called Drink and Dive. We basically have a foolproof system called 'Learn diving in 7 hours'. Obviously that's not seven hours in one day. But seven one-hour sessions spread over a week. Lots of clients don't understand this, and so book their stay for three days only. Then complete only half the course, and then have to come back and redo all seven sessions at another time again. As you can see it's a foolproof system, from the commercial side of it. Our learning process is great. The first session is in a bathtub. The second one is in a pool. Then we return you to the bathtub to get clean. Then we take you to a pool with seawater. Then back again to the bathtub to get cleaned. The sixth session is when you actually go into the deep blue sea. In the seventh session, we return you to the bathtub, because at Drink and Dive, hygiene is paramount. Now even if you don't grasp the rudiments of diving, by the end of the seventh session, you are a complete expert in the bathtub and more importantly, you're spanking clean. This brings me to my problem. I met this client called Susan, who is from Slovakia and we she was scheduled for a four day course, and when she realized that the diving course would not be completed, she flew into a rage, and demanded her money back. We tried to reason with her. We even tried to compromise by offering to let her keep a towel and a bathrobe, but she wouldn't listen. Now, she's left. But is in touch via email, and by touch I mean she's threatening legal action. I think I'm head over heels in love with her. But how do I pry our romance out of this awkward situation? After all, Drink and Dive is my life. By the way, after all this, she kept the bathrobe, but returned the towel. We are communicating via the internet, but she's constantly calling me things of which the least insulting were 'back portions of a donkey' and a collective combination of putrid waste matter mixed with evil duplicity beyond the capacity of actual human beings. However, since she begins her emails with the word 'Dear', I feel all is not lost. Please help.

Trevlin Phillip Finn

Your determination is admirable, even though all virtue has clearly passed you by. After thoroughly examining the evidence on display, I can only say this, and I mean this lure clients, and then ensure they don't get their money's worth is extremely admirable. And the trapdoor you have laid for coercing them to return to complete the course, thus doubling your financial well-being, is to be truly admired. However, what is truly satanic and must be condoned, is your brazen self-belief into believing Susan and you could still work things out. And this presumption is based purely on a free bathrobe that you were forced to loan her! So, in terms of evil and corrupt practices, I think you have all the bases covered. Which brings us to your present condition of desperately seeking Susan! Having conned her once, and then trying to double con her later, you are now in a new relationship with her. One in which you love her, and she for her part wants to spew venom on you, start criminal proceedings against you, so that you are never heard off again. At the moment there seems to be only three ways for you to put a smile on her face and they are, if (a) you get hit by a truck, (b) drown in the sea, and (c) after getting hit by a truck and drowning in the sea, you get hit by truck again. You could write a detailed apology and refund her money to her. That could be one way of doing things. But on the other hand, why spoil a good thing? I mean you have

P.S.: You do get one clean thumbs-up for hygiene, though.

♥

I was born and raised in England. In the country of Worcester a town called Western Super, Mare. Since I work with an M.N.C., I got transferred to Mumbai. And that's where my girl problem started. I've tried to date various girls, but every time I make a little headway, I ran into the same roadblock. Pronunciation. It all started with the first girl I dated in India, Roopanjali. She was a perfectly nice girl. Young, pretty, with a settled job. She was worldly wise, had travelled the globe, but then when we were about to get intimate, she mispronounced the word 'develop'. The way she said it, she stressed on the first part, i.e., a loud 'dev' then a missing 'o' followed by a short sharp 'lop'. So it sounded like 'dddevolop'. I found this as a huge turn off, and dropped her like hot 'patatoe'. By the way that's another word she couldn't pronounce. Her 'patatoe' came out as 'pataattoh'. Obviously, after this I was on my guard. If you know what I mean. Then, I found the ravishing Suneeta. Suneeta was again everything help thing' and so on. However, this is what happened during the workshop. There were about twenty people in the class. The teacher began by mispronouncing both 'personality' (he split the word making it 'personal—ity'), as well as 'dddevelopment'. I was reeling in the aisle. Then Suneeta raised her hand, and asked a question on child-development. Except she said 'ddevelopment'. The last syllable sounding like the mint I was choking on when I heard her mispronounce the word. Then the whole class joined in, mispronouncing all kinds of words, along with what used to be... 'development'. 'Riposte' became 'ripostey', 'parental' became 'parentaal', 'guinea pig' became 'jinny pig', 'personal' became 'personaaal' and worst of all the famous social scientist Carl Jung (pronounced as Yung), was called by the Hindi equivalent, for war. Suffice to say, that I literally passed out. Can you please explain to me why perfectly well-educated, well-adjusted young ladies like Roopanjali and Suneeta , can't pronounce everyday words like 'develop' properly. I'm so turned off that I haven't dated a girl in the last three months. I seem to have a better time off it on Facebook, where they all at least can spell, but don't have to be heard. I'm really suffering. I've lost all confidence in Indian girls and pronunciation. Please

My brother, I feel your pain. As you described all those words to me, I cringed with each mispronunciation. I've been through all these bumps in the road myself. If it's any comfort to you, you are just in transit. I permanently live here. I have done so all my life. Along with nose hair and racist views, I found mispronunciations to be the biggest deal breakers myself. In time as my nasal cavity became more empathetic, and as I realized that all human beings are bigots, and that's a non-negotiable, I was able to adjust to the first two infractions. But mispronunciations still scare the hell out of me. Oh, and that word 'develop', that needs to be banned. It's destroying more relationships, than religion, the municipal corporations, and global warming collectively. It's almost a given, an Indian home truth, along with leaving front doors open, answering mobile phones at dinner tables, and not knowing the name of the Governor of one's state.

In the survey done by Glaab and Gokhale, for the *Linguistic Almanac* (global edition) way back in October 2011, less than 0.35 per cent of all Indians could pronounce the word 'develop' correctly. The only other described. A girl I once dated, on my birthday famously said, 'See how those makko (macho) men with sworeoeds (swords) and dddeveloped (developed) bodies stand'. It was the first time I cried in public as an adult since my grandmother's funeral. Now Manaav, while there is no cure and little hope for this audio catastrophe, I found one process, slightly helpful. In one word, scrabble. Keep a Scrabble board ready for use at home, work, and I dare say in your car. Immediately after meeting a girl you may fancy lure her into a game of Scrabble. 'Develop' in some form will appear very soon, I assure you. Moreover, one hour of Scrabble, will both expose and examine her. Once more than three words are mispronounced, you know it's a dead end. However, bear in mind that Scrabble will provide you with the slimmest of hopes, a very small flickering light at the end of the tunnel, an extremely faint echo of a minimal nano heart-beat, that you may one day run into the girl of your dreams. Who as defined by a Desi version of Welster's would be 'a girl who can actually pronounce the word "develop"'.

All the best, in solidarity,
Cyrus

Well that's me with chess. No, really. When I was young I'd sleep with my chessboard. Now I've grown out of it of course. Although I do have a bed shaped like a knight, and a bedspread made of the squares from a chessboard. At the age of eleven, I was diagnosed with severe indigestion, from swallowing two Rooks without water. Of course, I've stopped all that crazy behaviour and now stick to Pawns. They are smaller, more edible and above all, and this is most crucial, leave no after taste. And as far as drinking chess goes? I'm obviously still working on that. But enough about me. Let me tell you about my love problems. I'm in love with this girl, who I met on the chess circuit. That is, we both play tournaments. I won't give you too many details, but she's ranked no. 4 in India, and I'm ranked no.7 in India. But here is the real issue. She's ranked no.4 in the men's category. When we first met I was ranked no.6, and she had not even participated in the men's lineup. So, we started dating and since we shared a common interest (actually two)—mosaic gardens and chess—we obviously started playing a lot of chess with each other. It was such that, after a party, where other couples would get amorous, we would actually go back to my place and make some moves. Moves on the gained enough confidence to start playing on the men's circuit. And as it happens in 'B' movies, in her very first match she got me as an opponent and finished me off in sixteen straight moves to a standing ovation by all three people present to witness the feat. She, her mother and me. We are still together, but of late she's appearing to become more and more arrogant. She makes me hold her bag at tournaments. Which in itself is not so bad, but to have to do so while playing a chess match at the same time is downright humiliating. All decisions are made by her. She acts like I'm an employee, and a very basic level one at that. She also tweeted a picture of me losing to her, with a suggestion that I should find a third category to compete in, as the male and female ones were far beyond my capacity. Sometimes I want to break up, but she won't allow it. On the circuit, I'm forced to stare at my toes permanently to avoid tension. I heard you have a similar problem with your wife, so maybe you could help?

Yours truly, let's call me Vishy,
The Second Coming

Dear 'The Second Coming',

May I begin by telling you that I'm not in the same

extremely hushed tones, that she can be quite dominating. And just in case she reads this, may I add, in a really pleasant, charitable sort of way. Mr... errm... Coming, your problem mirrors the views of Rome's greatest Orathor Cicero P. Braganzo. For years, as a young man Cicero was the steeple chase-cum-obstacle race champion of Rome. After marriage his wife, Bertha the bountiful, would train with him. Soon using a new technique she would regularly beat him in the practice races. While Cicero swerved and swayed his way over various obstacles (such as three dead men, an elephant, a Trojan horse, two elephants, a wall), Bertha the bountiful simply used her ample girth to blast her way through. With this emasculation of Cicero, Bertha the bountiful's hubris grew as large as her ample frame. After months of menial subjugation, in which Cicero was made to wear high heels to cocktail parties, and had to carry his mother-in-law on his back so she could see the outskirt of the Mount Ve Surius and play the role of the dining table at family functions, Cicero hit on an ingenious trick to wrest back the initiative from Bertha the bountiful. He ran away to a very small village called Amora, in modern day Spain. Now Mr Second my friend, far be it for me to tell you the same. First, I don't think exactly the same as a mongoose with a snake. And sadly for you, she's the mongoose. Winning respect back only really happens in politics. Since you may never beat her in chess in the future, I think, Mr Second Coming, Sir, you need to bow out gracefully from this one. If you do insist on trudging on, may I suggest you start on a new activity, one in which, she may never be able to displace you in. Such as silence, or losing hair, or coughing or even dog walking. (Mind you in the last one please stick to little dogs only.) So let's toss it back to you, Secondbhai, change the lane or leave the pool.

Yours sincerely,
Cyrus

♥

A girl in my campus keeps staring at me. I tried to talk to her on Facebook. But I wrote something stupid and ruined it. She didn't chat with me after that. Somehow, I got her phone number and texted her, but she didn't reply. Recently, I came to know that she has a boyfriend outside the campus. So I have now stopped making eye

Dear Max Confused,

Eye contact is huge in most cultures. In ancient Persia, eye contact led to war. In ancient Egypt, eye contact meant you had to offer marriage. So you know what that tells you. Egypt was worse off than Persia. She has a boyfriend so she's avoiding any official contact. But eye contact is eye contact. She's persisting, which means she is scaring you but not letting you close. Give her the ignore, see if that breaks her icy demeanour. By the way, the last one is from ancient China, my favourite ancient culture.

Cyrus

♥

I have a few questions for you. The first question is who are you? The next is what do you do? The third is can you help me meet girls? Of course, this answer will depend on what you do, and who you are. My final question is if you can help me meet girls, could you give me a timeline? As in how long will it take? You see, I'm keen to get married by the age of twenty-five. I'm seventeen right now, engineering colleges, I'm told, meeting girls is confined to when, mothers, grandmothers or sisters visit you. I'm average looking but have a great IQ. My hobbies include travelling, fishing, and Facebook-ing. I haven't yet gone fishing, as there is no sea as yet in Lucknow. But I've read a lot of hobbies of people in the Facebook, and find that fishing is mentioned by lot of people, and it makes the user sound really cool. One more thing I'd like to mention, since we're on the subject of fishing, I don't like eating fish. And I'm allergic to shell fish. I think it's important that I come clean, and pour everything out before you, so that we're all cool. Cool?

Yours hopefully.
Emil

How do I put this correctly? I can't answer everything. For that you have Google, or that fellow on that English news channel. Your questions range from the innocent to the absolute absurd. Instead of some of them you might as well ask me to name 233 labourers who worked on building the Suez Canal. Anyone who really knows me will know, I'd be able to name only about nineteen of forced to answer your questions. What do I do? Well, I think the earlier answer covers this one too quite succinctly. Your next question, is the most important one any man can ask another man, after 'Is your sister married?' The long answer will take me pages to write, and days for you to decipher. So let me take the easy route. Let me give you the short answer to your most important query of, 'Can you help me meet girls?' The answer to that is a resounding 'NO!'. In fact no one can help you meet girls. Okay, that's not strictly true. There are people in certain professions who can, but they are difficult to reach at this precise moment. You then demand a timeline? Well, I can't help you meet girls. But the good news is, you've earned a timeline. And that is the rest of your life! From Hiawatha to Himesh Reshammiya, men are always trying to meet girls throughout their lives. It's an ongoing process, like an app that you need to constantly update. Emil, I will tell you this though. Girls luckily are found everywhere, on the road, at bus stops, on pavements, in buildings, on bridges, under bridges, at street corners, in restaurants, at shopping centres, in correctional facilities, in clubs, in courts, on maidens, in car parks, at aquariums, at picnics, in lifts, in factories, in educational institutions,

23½ Ways to Make a Girl Fall For You

Emil, I hope this adequately answers your questions, as vaguely, as is humanly possible. I implore you, young man don't keep scores of all your expenses. As their memories may make you quake in fear at a later date, which should be about ten or so years later, most possibly in the month of June. For further details, please read this whole book twice. Then write back to me and tell me what I've forgotten

All the best,
Cyrus

♥

Dear Cyrus Sir,

I was infatuated with an old friend. I always held back my feelings because I didn't want to ruin our friendship. I gave her hints and then got away from the whole situation as I freaked out. She didn't come back. Should I continue hoping that someday she may come back or just move on?

Yours sincerely,
Jimmy Anderson

Dear Mr Jimmy Anderson,

straighter one. What's the point of being half-hearted? With hints you can never be sure. You should have been straight up. I mean you still can locate her and give a last try. Although the timing is all wrong now, so I'd advise against it. Instead of looking for reverse swing with an old ball, why not move on and opt for a new ball?

Yours sincerely,
Cyrus Sir

♥

I think my friend's wife is having an affair. Every time I go out of town, errm.. I mean every time he goes out of town, she's out partying. Word gets back to him, and to me, but first to him, after which only it also gets back to me that she's been out painting the town. And it doesn't matter what day of the week it is. If he's out of town on a Monday, then she's out of her mind rocking away all Monday night. I mean who goes out on a Monday night? Even most barber shops are closed! I'm sure you are saying that's not enough, and that you need evidence. You people are all the same, always going on and on about evidence.

An obvious ploy to throw me off the scent. So obviously, it's actually quite infantile a ploy really. Of the two guys, one is already having an affair with my cousin's friend's brother's wife, so that cancels him out. The other guy, the second one is a known predator, and I've had my eye on him for a long time. Of course, only after my friend had his eye on this guy, and then quite naturally guided my eye to the same guy, his eye had been trained upon. My wife is very smooth. And by my wife, I obviously mean my friend's wife, who is almost like my own wife, but really is, clearly his. She makes sure they party in the suburbs, in a place that I would never frequent. Please help me, help him to catch this woman, and unveil the truth. My happiness depends on it. And by now I'm sure you follow that by my happiness, I mean our happiness. And by our, I'm actually leaning more towards his, my friend's happiness. Please advice accordingly with several options. Also since he's really busy with work right now, I thought I should write on his behalf.

Mr Durga Prasad

Mr Durga Prasad,

really. If only husbands and wives had the same concern, love, regard, and affection for each other, as you have for your friend. I do hope the feeling is reciprocated, and that when your wife steps out to have an affair, it may only be down under your friend's watchful, keen, and observant eagle eye. Now it pains me a lot to tell you, and by you, I mean your friend, that I don't believe in all this cloak and dagger. I did however find Henry VIII's approach quite fascinating. If he felt a wife was cheating on him, he had her beheaded. And he didn't waste time on evidence. If a friend told him so, that was evidence enough. Of course, he later started abusing this privilege. And started executing his wives for many innocuous reasons. One of them being, he really had nothing to do on a Tuesday. (Some critics say that this wasn't the only day). However, times have changed. And today, a beheading would be stretching it. A nose pull in the modern context should suffice. So, Mr Durga Prasad, I have only one piece of advice for you and that is to get her to level with you. And by you, I mean your friend. Although let me clarify, by her, I mean, her. A good old face to face, heart to heart, with obviously a couple of inches breathing space in between, is underrated and hence underused these days. Lay out all your evidence, sinister tricksters, the old heart to heart can really set everything right one way or another. I guess if it worked for good ole Henry VIII, why can't it work for you? And by you, I mean him and not you. Although it would be nice if you heard the whole thing from him. And by him, I mean him and by you, I mean you. It's called being open-hearted. Try it, please!

Yours sincerely,
Cyrus

♥

I hate Facebook. Really, that's my problem! I hate it. I hate it the day it was born. I should have known better. How can you trust a thing which has both the words 'face' and 'book' in it? Really, if I didn't have so many friends, I'd disown it. You know what? I will drown it someday, I swear. Yup, three things I have to do: give up my material possessions, turn vegetarian and give up Facebook. Okay, maybe I was being hasty. Forget about the vegetarianism. But the other two? Coming Soon! Now let me explain to you the exact turn of events. My Mom's the same likes and passions, which could be summed up in one word. Facebook. Okay, two words with a hyphen in between. And we ended the evening after friending each other successfully. At the end of the evening, I dropped a Gulaab-jaam from my plate, and it seems to land into lots more. Gulaab-jaam. Only what I thought was the Gulaab-jaam mother lode, was in actuality another girl called Freya. Now Freya picked up the Gulaab-jaam, separated it from herself and handed it back to me. You know when you have those cinematic, romantic moments where two sets of eyes meet in a loving gaze over a dropped something or the other? Well this was a version of that moment. Except, only her eyes had the loving gaze. My loving gaze was reserved for my beloved Gulaab-jaam. Freya, convinced that cupid had struck, now started pestering me to friend her on Facebook. I tried to cry, but no tears would come out at that juncture. They never come out when you need them, you know. Instead, I came up with a cunning plan. I told Freya I had disconnected myself from all social networks as I was leaving the country on a mission for many years. Of course, this made no sense, as the people who leave their home countries on mission for many years are precisely the people who desperately a Gulaab-jaam can be sisters? Who cares, how come? The problem is Farida didn't reply to my posts, so obviously the sisters talked. And now I really want to poke that Mark Zuckerberg fellow and how! So, can you tell me how I can undo this damage, and also unhate Facebook? I really like Farida, but I feel I need a better explanation then the one I posted.

Yours sincerely,
Aparajit@TheDemolitionMan.com

The truth is that we're drowning here. Freya's upset, Farida's upset, and once I sell 10,000 copies of this book, Facebook will be upset. Let's turn to China's very own, Sun-Yat-Sen, who, in a letter to his grandnephew in Calcutta, Prosenjit Sen, pointed out the way back homeward after the damage is done in three simple but clear steps. Keep in mind that the topic they were dealing with was baldness. Baldness in teenagers, more specifically. Baldness in female teenagers, namely Prosenjit Sen's sister, Ronjona Sen. The steps were: (a) hide, (b) deny, and (c) wear a cap, and deny. I want you to borrow liberally from the great Sun-Yat-Sen. But for that to happen I need you to pretend, need to get in touch with both, and deny the sequence of events. Blame the Gulaab-jaam. Blame the politics of Calcutta. Blame Sun-Yat-Sen! But deny rejecting Freya. Be firm in your denial, but at all times be apologetic for any misunderstanding. The great thing about words is they mean different things in different contexts. Like in cricket, a batsman who is 'out' is 'in' the pavilion. Third, you need to wear a cap, now I'm not sure how that will help, but since it was advocated by the great Sun-Yat-Sen (himself a great hit with the ladies), I say let's do it anyway. So, you may be drowning, but there's always a rope... and a cap. As for Facebook, isn't that why they tell you not to judge a Facebook applicant by her face? Hello!

Yours sincerely,
Cyrus Broacha

I recently bought a copy of *Modern Romance* by American Indian comedian Aziz Ansari. But I couldn't understand anything, as he failed to localize the book to suit the Indian tastes. I mean typical Indian cities like Mumbai, Delhi, and

Williams and Barack Obama are other case studies. And please don't tell me Ansari was born in the USA. That's no excuse in my books. I'm twenty-two years old and am particularly prone to using my fingers to entice women. And by fingers I meant texting. Could you please help me with this 'texting' phenomena? But please give examples from an Indian context. And when replying to me, please don't use an American accent. Fake accents can be quite irritating. Now, the three things I want you to reply to me with are: (a) texting initial messages, (b) profile pictures, and most important, (c) the kind of reply to be replied, after one has sent many messages and finally got a reply, which you now need to reply to. Can you please clarify the above for me?

Mr Bagchi

Wow! That's an unusual request. You basically want me to clean up Aziz Ansari's book. May I remind you, he got paid three-and-a-half million dollars for it. This means if he paid, one lakh readers 350 dollars each to read his book, he'd still be paid more money than me. So obviously I'm devasted and can only write the next paragraph, next week.

of my ability. (Just leaving a little slack, so I can withstand the pressure.) To do this, I decided to Google Aziz Ansari, here's what the internet threw up.

There are over four lakh Aziz Ansaris (rightfully he should share his book fee with all other Aziz Ansaris; three-and-a-half million not looking so great now.)

There are 267 books with the title *Modern Romance*. Although one is about the end of the Roman Empire, clearly a spelling error. And quite possibly the one you were unfortunate enough to peruse.

Aziz has just been commissioned to write a sequel to his first book for a fee of five million dollars.

Obviously, I'm devastated and am still digesting this unsavory news. So please bear with me as I postpone the next paragraph to late next week.

(LATE NEXT WEEK)

Brother, I'm back, and I've decided not to let this Aziz Ansari destroy our relationship. And more importantly, on a personal level, destroy me. So let's look at your three queries. Initial messages in foreign conditions can allow you to go straight to the point. A common example is 'Hey, how's it hanging?' Here no specific item is mentioned as and would be hell-bent on a search to find the 'danglee', so to speak. We are a literal people. Hence, when we say someone's 'off', we literally mean he's no longer 'on' and cannot be reactivated. Meaning, he's passed away. For a foreigner, 'He's off' simply means a person has moved from his previous geographical location, and is at present in a constant state of movement. For e.g., 'He's off for a run'. For initial messaging, in our conditions, it is better to start with a traditional Indian greeting like 'Namaste'! Thus, conveying the three most important tenets of Indianism, as pronounced by scientists Kopke and Kazi, that of being a traditionalist. Furthermore, a conservative and god-fearing person. And also that you live with your parents and are not averse to doing all the latest Bollywood dance numbers in a public space. Keep in mind, the 'Namaste' is a standalone greeting. Don't add other words. After, sending it, wait for her to 'Namaste', you back. Thus conveying to you that she too is a traditional, conservative, god-fearing girl who is well-versed with the current Bollywood dance numbers, and that she will be paid to perform them in public with you. If she fails to answer your 'Namaste', consider the whole thing off. By 'off' I mean in the foreign context, out of your reach and gone, not the Indian meaning. If to your reply of what to reply, should you choose to reply to her reply, is simple. You don't! The general reply of three applies here. If three texts aren't replied to, she's off. Again, not off in the foreign sense, exactly. But, somewhere between the foreign and Indian interpretation, 'She's off', as in she's gone away from her last known position and location, and so is actually dead to you, yet still not 'dead' dead. That is not expired, fine. Kaput! In India, we don't believe in closures. When we want someone, we chase them obsessively. And when we don't want them anymore, we ignore them and run the other way. It is in our oriental DNA and culture. We avoid confrontation and collision. It's why our batsmen, in cricket, prefer the leg glance to the hook shot. So, never confront, play to your local strengths and back off if not replied to. And by back off, I mean both 'back' and 'off' in the foreign context here; geographically move away as far as possible from the girl

To your second query, brother, profile pictures are a complicated lot. For Indian conditions, avoid your present normal portrait picture at all costs. This is because we are not particularly photogenic people. And second, bear in mind that we Indians and specially males, tend to have very favourite (e) paralyzed! But thankfully there are two words in the Indian dictionary that will help you in this crisis. The words are photo-shop. Technology, and especially digital technology, was invented by the Indians, off the Indians, and most definitely for the Indians. Use technology to clean up your mess. But please never let her see the real you. Such a sight is subject to severe market risks, which in turn are subject to many different variables, including, but not limited to, lighting, background, genetics, the theory of relatively and mood swings. All this is far beyond the capacity of a third party to put right. No matter if the third party is one of the four lakh Aziz Ansaris. By the way, I've just heard that Aziz Ansari's book *Modern Romance* is to be made into a Bollywood blockbuster movie. For which he will be paid ten million dollars as fee. Thus, I'm sure you'll excuse me, as I'm feeling damp and dull, and am contorting my lower body in a desperate aim to ease the pain, and must excuse myself from any correspondence till the week after early next week.

Yours sincerely,
Cyrus (far less, far, far less than three-and-a-half million dollars) Broacha

requests his publisher, to maintain the next two pages as blank pages, as a mark of respect to this author's bewilderment, anguish, and abject horror. Furthermore, readers are requested to maintain a two minute silence, before reading further. Sorry, make that three minutes. Please. One minute for each

♥

I was in a relationship for a couple of years. Then I broke up because she was weak. Later, I lost my love for her. But, she still loves me a lot. I'm looking forward to dating her again. Should I date her again?

Master V.

By very weak, what do you mean exactly? That she couldn't do a 400 squat? That she caught a cold every time she went swimming? Or that if you poked her with your finger she'd fall down? Having dropped her, you now want to be magnanimous and take her back. What an act of charity! What a humane gesture!! No, you shouldn't date

23½ Ways to Make a Girl Fall For You

♥

I have been in coma for the past two years. However, thanks to my father's perennial coughing, I woke up last month. A miracle of modern science! I was completely hale and hearty. And although I can touch my toes, water the plants, and use the bathroom on my own, one thing has changed in the past two years. Before the coma, I was dating a girl called Superna. Yet, when I came to, I was told I was dating a girl called Sugandha. In fact, Sugandha came to the hospital to take me home, but I had no idea who she was. My memory is fine. I still remember all the lyrics of, 'Saawan Mai Lag Gayi Aag', my favourite song. Feel free to quiz me as my memory is intact. When I was about to slip into coma, Scahin was about to play and last test. When I came out of the coma I was told that he wouldn't be playing his 300th, as I had hoped. All my organs are working. Yet, everyone calls my girlfriend Sugandha. My question is where is Superna? Is Sugandha, Superna? And if that is so, then was there ever a Superna? If so, why is Superna missing? Why do my

Congratulations on coming out of the coma. Please convey my congratulations to your dad too, on a job well done! What I can't understand is that, don't you have any pictures of Superna? Some digital proof? Emails from the female, so to speak. If so, does Superna look like your girlfriend Sugandha? On the other hand, after investigating the empirical evidence at hand, in a thorough, decisive and refined manner, not crossing more than seven seconds, let me tell you that with your resurrection you have been given a new lease of life. Embrace that! You may be stuck with the same set of parents, but looks like lucky new you, now has been given a new girlfriend. Most men I know would readily go into coma for the same. So, is there no way you could be happy and content with your fresh, new friend? I know you may pine for Superna, but if Superna is Sugandha, then you've got a new Superna, while still retaining the old Superna. Except your new Superna is now called Sugandha, and no longer Superna. Besides, god gave you your life back, so let's not get greedy, and ask for everything. Nobody gets everything. Except maybe the early Elvis. Sugandha, Superna, Mahendra, Narendra,

Just to be safe, don't call Sugandha, Suparna.

♥

It has been brought to my attention that you are in the business of advising people on how to gain success in romance. If this is so, can you please tell me how this works? How do you monetize your business? Do you get paid per letter? Or how may words do you write? Or on the success or failure of the advice? Which brings me to the tax implications? Is there an affixed rate? Do you accept cash? Do you have to pay service tax? And what are your working hours? I ask you all this because I too am very good at helping people with their romantic problems. So, I just needed to know if I could monetize my talent in the way that you have, and thus enjoy material success. Yet, even you and me, people who help other people in love, even if we have our own share of problems. Mine is really strange. You see, as a dentist I'm constantly dealing with open mouths. This has opened up a whole cesspool of ugly truths about oral hygiene. Mouths are dreadful. Women are no exceptions. The lack of flossing and brushing means eight tubes, endless bits of gauge and various chemicals, inside her mouth, means Ms Classy lady smells like the wrong end of her pet poodle. I am so ruffled by all this that I just can't get myself to kiss a girl I'm with. I just can't do it. I try, but I can't. What I've been exposed to has scared me and scarred me! Can you please help me get over my kissing complex? And one more thing, do

Dr Doubtfire

Dear Dr Doubtfire,

What a sweet and thoughtful letter. And all these questioning on the romance query industry, while absolutely infantile, is simultaneously utterly charming. Let me tell you that I'm not part of any guild as yet. Also, as the number of romance query letter writers, pan India, stands only at a resolute number of nine writers, we can't be considered an industry. You should know that to be an industry you must have at least ten members. And let's never ever talk about service tax and cash or cheques in a public forum. As far as I know, my payment is in the form of service to humanity. Which, as you have probably guessed by now, stands at a little less than very little, which brings us to

Valley Civilization. While coitus had been invented (the exact date is unclear), and that invention claimed by the Chinese (thus giving them a head start and a lead in the population, a lead they still enjoy today but perhaps not for long), kissing was unheard of. Men used their lips only to make guttural, vulgar sounds (which may or may not have led to the birth of the German language). While women of that time used their lips to warm other women of the impending presence of men. Or if the men came too near, then they learnt to use their lips to spit on them. An act which obviously encouraged the men and led to the birth of the art of pressing. (In which we Indians hold the lead, as far as international standards go.) Irritated that men seemed to get more out of this pressing, and disgusted by their awful audio capacity, Harappan women hit back. They silenced the males by locking lips, during all bodily functions. And here I'm told (very softly), ALL bodily functions. So please don't ask me to further elaborate. Men compromised and accepted their lot, and kissing grew in practice and length as years went by. My point to you Dr Doubtfire is the Harappans invented kissing in around 12,000 BC. Yet, brushing of teeth and the concept of oral hygiene only came to our shores with to tonnes of raw saliva slipping out of their cupboards and onto your gloved hands. So what? Learn from our elders. And whose older than a Harappan lady called 'Paravatibai', who would currently be 14,407 years old. The Moldavians have a superb saying which is both unpronounceable and unreadable, yet it sums up the way forward. The saying goes thus, 'There is no love without a kiss Abe'. Some of this is difficult to translate. For instance, nobody knows who 'Abe' is. He or she remains unidentified. However, the kiss and love thing is inseparable. So, get off your high horse-cum-dental-seat thing, and allow yourself the unparalleled, exquisite thrill of the kiss. A word of caution though, always carry your own mint. Oh and no, we don't, now and forever, entertain interns.

Cyrus

I love a girl from my college. We know each other for ten years. She never had the same feelings for me. I tried expressing my feelings for her on several occasions, but she made fun of it and ignored. Last year, she started texting her to make up her mind and accept my proposal. But four months ago, she blocked all communication channels between us. I don't know what is going on in her life. How do I communicate with her?

Ace

I'll tell you exactly what Jimmy Bharucha, 'ACE' dog trainer, told my Beagle Figaro, when Figaro tried to steal food off the table. 'NO!!' The word is 'no', and it means basically a negative result as in you can't, won't, shan't, mustn't. She made fun of you, rejected you, and now cut off all communication with you. If one pigeon had done the same to another pigeon, the rejected pigeon is not known for its brains and intellect. If it can understand… we Indian men have to understand the meaning of 'NO!!' If you're having trouble still, I can recommend a suitable

Yours sincerely,
Cyrus

already married. So I told a friend of Girl to tell this to Girl. But Girl on her own found out, and is now with Boy D. Just within one day. I'm waiting like idiot in line, twenty-seven months! Boy B is gone, Boy C is on way out. Boy D is in. But how long for me? She knows me, and I know her. So, we know each other, but how long? How many more boys will she forever find? My patience is giving out? But I'm falling on her badly. What to do about such situation? Do give agreeable solutions, please.

Myself Tomboy

It's just amazing. Your English is as pathetic as your punctuation is spot on! How can someone with such a poor command over a language, punctuate so perfectly? It boggles the mind! Also, I don't think Tomboy would be appropriate. It's a term used for girls and generally not for boys. I'm not quite sure, but may be try Tomgirl? Your problem however seems pretty serious. You seem to be beaten to the draw by Boy B, C, and now even D. That's the bad news. The good news is that the English alphabet (which you have vaguely used) has only twenty-six letters. So in about twenty-two more boys, your number you and your feelings, then how is she to love you back? To make matters clear, I imagine there is a bust of a famous man, outside her house. Everyday in her periphery she may see the statue, but how is she to know that this very same statue, loves her? If the statue doesn't have the common sense and decency to interact with her. But, let's not blame the statue. It's just a statue. It has a valid excuse. Immobility! That's the very essence of being a statue. It's the badge of all the statue tribe. But you, presumably, are more than just a bust. So, what's holding you back? On all my Thursday morning lectures at Vilson college (spelt with a 'V'), I'm constantly crying myself hoarse saying, if you like someone you need to interact with the said person. You can just exist, and expect a romance to occur. This may work for amoeba, but humans need to know. Your friends don't need to know. Your parents don't need to know. But 'Girl' needs to KNOW!

Contrary to what early medical practitioners felt, this patience game is highly overrated. If you need me to explain further, I'm sorry to tell you, it's time for me to play statue and you to be more than just a bust. Play to your strengths, maybe? Email her and astound her with your perfect punctuation. But it pains me to tell you, please let

And now to relieve the monotony of only men writing letters, a girl comes along. And you can tell it's a girl from the perfect punctuation.

♥

I love a guy who's four years elder to me. He says he's too busy because his exams are going on. But I always see him online on Facebook or Whatsapp. He doesn't even reply to my texts. I love him a lot and it hurts when he's online and doesn't reply to me. I feel he doesn't love me. I'm confused. Please help.

Yours truly,
Ms Confused

Dear Ms Confused,

I'm so confused that you are confused. He's not interested in you, it's so clear. So where is the confusion? Didn't you learn anything from the pigeon explanation? What about the dog trainer? 'No', in any language means 'NO'. You can't force love. It's against the law if you do. You've given it a fair shot. Just like the CPI party did in politics. Cut your

23½ Ways to Make a Girl Fall For You

Please, before I begin to tell you my situation in minute eye-catching detail, let me warn you that in my second standard I got the 'Best-behaved child' in my class award. The next year I got the award again, the 'Best-behaved child in the second standard', once again. Although, by then I should have been in the third standard. But till today, no one has quite explained to me why that didn't happen to me. I'm telling you this because I've always come across as a courteous person, well-behaved and well-adjusted! (Although now this repeating of the second standard memory is clouding my well-adjusted, adjustment!) I have no police case or court case appearance in my entire history of being a human being. And that includes my two years in the second standard. (Still don't understand why that happened). Very often, when I have a room I can hear various voices in the background saying, 'There goes a very well-adjusted, courteous, and suitably behaved man'. I hope you are convinced by this slew of facts that you are dealing with a very courteous and well-behaved person. Please also note I used the words, 'dear' and 'please' at the top of this letter. This brings me to me in the centre and Parul on the right. Parul and I are friends. We've been sharing the cab for over a year now. Not continuously throughout the year, more like in the evenings, on working days. Last week, on the long drive back, Barry cracked a joke. I liked it so much that I grabbed his thigh and squeezed it. Which would have been okay if it was Barry's thigh. Actually I had inadvertently squeezed Parul's thigh. Not only did I squeeze her long left upper leg, but I slapped it twice, and then squeezed it thrice while doubling up in peals of laughter. She screamed and threatened me. Being the gentleman that I am, I tried to reassure her by saying I would pay her fare for that cab ride. Finally, Barry, SriKrishna, the cabbie and all the honking cars with abusive drivers behind us, convinced her to not file a police case. From the next day she stopped coming on the evening ride. Which made sense as it was a Saturday. But the Monday which followed confirmed this fact. However, from my side a strange thing happened. I sprouted a love boil! No, really I developed this boil in my neck, which simultaneously coincided with me suddenly having great tender feelings towards Parul. I love her! I absolutely love her. But she walked out of my cab. I have her details. She's a 34-27-36. And I also have her phone

23½ Ways to Make a Girl Fall For You

While your letter seems perfectly clear, your diagram has left me, quite frankly, bewildered. In the diagram you appear to be sitting on top of the lady, in question. If it is so, it's a grievous fault of yours. And I will immediately recommend a whole list of lawyers that you need to get in touch with. Besides, in the front seat, the taxi driver appears to be on the left side of the car, while your friend SriKrishna, appears to be on the right side of the car. This leaves us with the two possibilities: (a) Your taxi driver owns the only left-hand-driven taxi-cab in Mumbai, or (b) You've accidentally reversed the cab occupant positions in your diagram. Which means Parul is on your left now and Barry is to your right. And you and I both know what this means. It means you molested Barry. It was Barry's thigh. Which means Parul is upset because you touched Barry. Which makes this a simple case of—homophobia! However, since you have your mind set on Parul, and not Barry, I'll ignore the diagram and stick to your note. Which, between you and me, appears to be a 'B flat'. My friend, first we must follow the advice of the mountaineer Dellio O. Berrande, who after climbing Mount K2, thinking it to be Nanda Devi, simply exclaimed in French, 'What's done is done?' (His application to rename K2 to Nanda down period. Try to send feelers, possibly through innocent bystanders like SriKrishna and Barry. Just convey your embarrassment and regret. You have to slowly convince Parul that you are the victim here. She should learn of how your confidence with women is shaken, of how you shaved your head and undertook a 'mannat' not to get married, till she forgives you. How you've spend seven months in Cambodia, working with a leper colony. How you plan in relinquishing life, including all dance forms, to become a Buddhist monk. How you shaved your eyebrows as penance. How you've given up cigarettes and alcohol (at least when consumed simultaneously). Let her get this feedback. Then obtain feedback of the feedback. If that feedback of the feedback sounds positive then you've got the kind of feedback that you will allow you a second innings. But, Mr Best-behaved, please, please don't try a direct approach. And never communicate with Parul through diagrams ever again.

Yours sincerely,
Cyrus

♥

nine kilos. Many people say I look like the rapper Snoop Dogg. Maybe because, I wear my hair long and maybe or my poor eye sight. I suffer from 'Rectinus Moravis'. Please don't bother looking that up. It's very rare, so rare that even Google couldn't 'Google' it. From an early age, due to my condition, my eye allows for too much light to pass through it. Three times the amount of light a normal person's eyes would experience. Thus, I'm forced to wear dark glasses, all the time. Due to this compulsory necessity, I can't tell day from night. And have often had my lunch at dinner time. It has also affected my work. I drew attention to myself as an architect, by my standalone style. None of my buildings have windows. This may explain why I've had to change them four times this year already. Also, I get cheated out of the 3-D experience in cinemas all the time. 3-D goggles are way too weak for me, so I pay extra for absolutely nothing. Thanks to spell-check, I am able to type this letter. But that can't help me with my dating issues. I'm sure by now you have figured it all out. I can't see girls! I mean I can see them, but not very clearly. Lunch dates are pretty much a nightmare. I spend the whole time looking down at my feet to avoid the blinding glare. And some time back, I asked a girl out,

I bang into the water cooler, I can hear hushed laughter and people exchanging money. I think they all bet on what I'm going to bang into next. The other side of this is I'm not able to tell how pretty my date is. I can see her form and figure, but for details I need the right amount of less light, and I need to stare at her face and body parts for more than seven consecutive minutes and no further than four-and-a-half inches away from her physical body. As you can well imagine, most girls are uncomfortable about this process, and very often my first date ends with a police complaint lodged by my date. Medically, I have got access to the best treatment available, but how do I convince a girl that I'm really like this on a first date? And how do I get her to respond well? Finally, how can I verify that she is pretty? And that she is in actuality a girl? Also, I may not be able to read your letter properly, but please don't let that stop you from writing.

Yours desperately,
Vir Sachdev

Dear Mr Vir Sachdev,

I hope you can read my reply. I've used the blackest typeset I could find. I also wrote this in almost complete

23½ Ways to Make a Girl Fall For You

'Rectinus Moravis' is to do with a detached rectum. And is prevalent only amongst the 'Ocaaru' tribe of Western Papua New Guinea. However, since you insist on having a poor eyesight, let's not dilly-dally and straightaway deal with your burgeoning problems. Sir, the best way to reach a girl, and give her an initial glimpse into your world (forgive the pun here please), is by providing her with a similar letter you sent me. Of course, please note down a couple of things, and these are very important things. Don't address this letter to me, address it to her. However, we also have a chicken and egg like situation. Which is, you are not sure what your date looks like or even have trouble confirming the gender? Well, for this you need to get a seeing guide dog. A well-trained German Shepherd using his nose should be able to confirm, what gender the person is. And he'll be able to convey the same to you by using the communication of touch. One lick for a girl, two licks for a boy, for example. And three licks for dinner. Yet the canine won't be able to confirm the prettiness quotient. After all, what's pretty for a German Shepherd, may not be the same for you. All kinds of misunderstanding may ensue. After 'Bulbul', the last thing you need is for your date to be a female but is, perhaps, the only conduct to clear vision for you. Only please make sure the said person doesn't: (a) sample the product, (b) share this information with others, or (c) turn mischievous and upload the videos of you at a date with a watermelon, unbeknownst to you. Now for the good news! While there is no doubt, that lack of vision is a hindrance is scanning a mate, it's a great help in keeping one over the years. After spending decades together, the less you can see of another, the better. In your particular case longevity in a relationship once properly scanned should be no real problem, given your unique situation.

Yours sincerely,
Cyrus

Please visit the western tip of the Fiji Islands to learn more about your disease, 'Rectinus Moravis'. I have seen pictures, and believe me, 'Rectinus Moravis' has nothing to do with the eye and nor should it ever be exposed to

♥

four feet eleven inches. Oh, and to reach this height, I have to arch my back and stand on my toes. I think girls don't seem to like short people. Very often they seem to miss me, literally. I'm worried about this tall dark handsome thing. Since I'm short, very fair, and sort of handsome, I seem to be inadequate to entice any girl. And please don't ask me to find shorter girls. All the shorter girls I know are eleven years old. Besides I don't like short girls. I like tall ones. Also, don't ask me to get a chin-up bar and do chin-ups. I did that for five years, and the only thing that seemed to grow was the chin-up bar itself. By the way, I have been on a few dates, let me share with you some of the highlights. One girl seriously asked me if I paid a half-ticket on the bus. Another asked me if everything was in proportion. A third agreed to a second date on the condition that I wore heels. I did. She didn't turn up. Please help me. So far all the advice I have ever got has been pretty much useless. You are my only hope.

Yours sincerely,
NotAmitabhBachchan@LambooDada.com

Dear Mr NotAmitabhBachchan@LambooDada.com,

You may be short, but your name is long! But I hear you.

you left out the important fourth quality—confidence. Women seem to be attracted to confidence. Now let us draw strength from the famous Iranian tightrope walker, Naseer Jalaabi. Naseer himself was just three feet seven inches. And this, at a time when there were no tape measures. Then, you simply made Naseer stand near the back of a six foot gelding. If he stood below the horse's tail he was considered short. If the horse consequently kicked him, he was short and injured. Jalaabi was so short that the horse's kick went over him. Yet Naseer Jalaabi became a celebrity at the Caliph's court. Instead of allowing himself to be ridiculed by both horses and human, he instead made sure he shot (spelled without the 'r') to prosperity and fame with a unique talent of his own. That of tightrope walking. That his third tightrope walk, ended in his untimely death, is another matter. Drunk with his own success, he attempted to walk across the city of Damascus crossing only on a tightrope. However, somewhere in the middle, this by now absolutely mad, egotist insisted that one end of the rope be disconnected from the pillar it was fastened to. Unfortunately, Naseer Jalaabi plunged forty-five feet to his untimely death. But, by then he had become so popular, that the parts of him

23½ Ways to Make a Girl Fall For You

ask for police protection, to stop adoring female fans from chasing him down. Now please Mr NotAmitabhBachchan@LambooDada.com, not for a minute am I suggesting you start mastering tightrope walking. And in fact, if we are both being perfectly honest here, let me implore you to avoid ropes altogether, forever. Except if you go bungee jumping. Instead learn from Naseer Jalaabi, and find some talent, which gives you newfound confidence and great self-esteem. And miraculously you will find the ladies coming. Here's my list of suggested talents: (a) juggling, (b) kabbadi, (c) singing, (d) Nintendo. Also here's my list of things you shouldn't pursue: (a) basketball, (b) swimming with sharks, (c) breeding Komodo Dragons in your home, (d) any sport that causes you to kneel or lie down, thus making you to appear even smaller. (Although why any sport that is about lying down or kneeling is still a sport, continues to remain a baffling mystery to me.) Mr NotAmitabhBachchan@LambooDada.com, I hope you've understood my point here, which is, find your inner Naseer Jalaabi. But always avoid Damascus, at all costs.

Yours sincerely,
Cyrus

complicated. I think I like them, but I can't tell if they are lying when they speak to me. My friend Faaju, says they lie all the time, but Faaju is also an idiot. He thought Siberia was the capital of China. Thank god I told him it was Hongkong, just before our big geography exam. See, I know when boys are lying, because our lips move from upto down. But when girls lie, I can't seem to tell. So please can you suggest how to find out if they are lying?

Yours sincerely,
Mikhaail

You have posed a very difficult question. A question that hasn't been answered in thousands of years, from the time primitive man brought home the hind, quarters of a dinosaur, and told his wife it was a rabbit for dinner. Telling a lie is an art. Catching a lie is an incomplete science. For instance, how do you know that I'm not lying? Frankly, you don't! The other day, I broke a traffic signal and told the policeman I was a heart patient. He charged me extra! The ancient Greeks followed the philosopher law of womankind, which stated that a woman would always join her eyebrows when she was in like a pneumatic drill while sleeping'. He then went on to enlist this sound, 'eeeeeeeeeeeee'. And he only stopped making this sound publicly after he was banned from all 'Page 3' parties! Of course, Methodus's own wife, to spite him, shaved off her eyebrows. And because he castigated her in public, she shaved off his eyebrows as well, while he was sleeping.

I get asked this 'lying' question many times, and I have lied so much while answering them that even I can't make head or tail of it anymore. Please prepare yourself that we all lie, women too. Some lies you'll catch, some you won't. Amongst the lies you should watch out for from girls are, 'I can drive, and I can also park a car', 'I like men with a sense of humour', and the one that makes me cringe, but you will have to hear sooner or later is, 'I love cricket'. What a lie!

Yours sincerely,
Cyrus

I have a swelling in my left thigh which goes away in the

hang on a minute. I just realized you are a love consultant. But please do me a favour and pass these other physical ailments of mine to your peers. Now that I've disturbed you, I might as well tell you of my 'girl' problems. I have the usual problems that all or most Indian men have. You know them by heart now, I'm sure. But I'll go on record anyway. First, no girl has the remotest idea I exist. Even if any girl does, she makes damn well sure that I don't have the faintest idea she exists. Further, I'm shy around girls and amphibians, although I don't always run away in fear from amphibians. And I can have great conversations with girls as long as they are in photographs. And, yes I have one ultra problem. That is even if you can suggest a way for me to break the glass ceiling, so to speak, let me also tell you that I'm very religious and I do everything, plan everything, adhere to everything according to what my Guruji says. Just to give you an example, yesterday my Guruji said stay away from water for twenty-four hours. So I haven't had a bath or a sip of water for a whole day. Of course, I did have four sweet lassis and three glasses of Tang at my best friend Kritin's wild birthday bash. And since I can hear you scoffing at all this, wait till you hear about the miracles my Guruji has performed. Do you know he

Guruji doesn't have FaceTime because something about his beard not fitting, but I definitely spoke to a Michael who sounded like an authentic American. Do you know my Guruji himself has discovered twenty-seven new animal species? All of which have been named after him such as The Ridley Turtle. (Yes, my Guruji's middle name is Ridley, or may be Turtle.) So when I meet my girl she has to follow what my Guruji says, or it won't work out. How can I ensure my girl will be loyal to my Guruji?

Debby Dibboo

Dear Debby Dibboo,

What a letter! So many questions. About your physical ailments, I'm sorry my peers won't be able to help you. And that's because my peers are all dog walkers, who unlike me are paid to do that service. And believe me I know all of them inside out. None of them have any medical qualifications. In fact, the whole lot has no qualifications whatsoever. I'd take this further and say that most of the dogs would have a better grip of all things medical. Now let's talk about Guruji. There are two broad categories of relationships. One in which the boy and the girl are self-sufficient in love, such as Romeo and Juliet, Laila and kids, sports, in-laws, Monopoly, and National Geographic, to name a few to help sustain them. This pairing enjoys a better success rate, although over the years, their individual relationships with National Geographic become the real defining ones. So, to answer your questions on Guruji, the truth is, it all depends on which girl lands up with you. If she's in the latter category you then are fine, Guruji is fine, and National Geographic is fine. If she's in the first category, you are doomed, Guruji is fine, and National Geographic is largely unused. It was the famous philosopher in me who said, and I quote myself here, 'The best relationships are not the ones where you change to accommodate others, but in fact, those in which you don't.'

I want to vent. I really don't want the answer. I just want to vent. I've vented a little on the internet. Check out my site www.cantfindanybridesobloodyunbelievable!.com. But most of my replies are very frivolous. 'Have you tried men?' 'Have you heard of plastic surgery?' 'From your profile picture I can see what the problem is!' These smart alecs are

Nipun was very upset with his wife of nine years who never informed him about her tailbone injury from her teen years. This has curtailed all her physical activity. So, the only activity in bedroom consists of him helping her off the bed! Here's what I want to vent about. Women want honesty, I'll give them honesty. They want sincere, truthful, straightforward partners, that's me in a nutshell. Let me now list what I want. Yes, it's time for us men to strike back. Newspapers, columns, books, podcasts, TV shows, spend hour upon hour telling you what women want. Let me bring on record, the truth from the other side. Here's what I want in a woman. You hear people say, looks are superficial, and don't be shallow. Well, those people are liars. Have you ever seen anybody go out of their way to marry an ugly girl? By chance? I don't mean arrangements amongst two families, I mean a male choosing an ugly female, because that's what he wants. Lies, lies, lies. What he wants, what I want, what every man who is not in a coma, or about to be eaten by an underwater predator wants is a good looking mate. And by good looking I mean, with striking physical attributes, and don't make me list and specify further. The word posterior, chest and hip to waist ratio will change the tenor of our conversation. But road, or if she runs down the same old lady in an effort to find a parking space. What I want is a girl who likes me, and likes the things I like! Whether it's football, scratching oneself, or massages. I want the woman to have that most noble of all qualities. Be all about me. My likes, my dislikes, my choices, my philosophy. In short, I want a female me who is pretty and madly in love with the male me. And who has made it her life's ambition to honour and serve me. So, no more lies, no more talks about compatibility and horoscopes, about sense of humour, and sensibility. I just want a girl who I can basically control, manipulate and get to suit me, and she has to be really hot. Ah! That felt good. The truth really sets you free. Thanks for letting me vent. And there's one more thing… she must allow me to vent without interrupting.

Yours sincerely,
cantfindanybridesobloodyunbelievable!.com

Dear cantfindanybridesobloodyunbelievable!.com,

I know you don't want a reply, so I'll keep this brief, and it's just a suggestion. I feel you should post this letter on your website and leave it there. I showed it to all the ladies I know, and it met with a very strange positive response.

girls. Once word gets around, about your demands, it's a clear given that women will flock back to you. Each and every one seeking your approval and consent. They will fight each other tooth and nail for your affections and attention. This will be true, as day follows night. As I write, oddly enough, there's a surge of feeling, a burst of affection, a great lump of want toward you. The very thought of ending my reply, and thus disconnecting from you is too hard to bear. I must reach for a tissue now, if you will please excuse me.

Cyrus Broacha

Please note my surname is normally spelt B R O A C H A. However, for you, and since you are clearly very special and a gift to womankind, Mr BRACHER is just fine, as that is who I am on alternate weekends.

♥

You must have heard of the famous astrologer, NKP? Yes? The one who wrote *Around the Moon but Only on Tuesdays*? His second book, *The Sun Says Stay South*, is soon to a leading astrologer, if not the world's best astrologer, have love problems. Let me share with you some details. Girl No. 1 and I went on a date to 'Imagica', which is a lovely amusement park, two hours west of Mumbai, if you are looking for it from Delhi. Girl No. 1 was a Libran. On that particular morning I checked our charts, and hers said 'be careful of accidents while driving a car'. So I cancelled the car option to Imagica. After some deliberation, I cancelled the bus option to Imagica. You see astrology is not an exact science. When the stars say car, they may interpret a bus as a big car. Why take a chance with the stars? When I suggested we walk the 120 km journey, initially she thought it was a joke. But that doesn't explain her violent attack on me with her huge handbag, with large metal attachments, roughly fourteen km into our stroll. Let's leave her aside and look at Girl No. 2. This Aquarian and I had a decent time for about three months. Then one particular Thursday, I stopped her from going to work. She had a super important meeting with prospective joint venture partners. But her forecast for the day made it abundantly clear that she could be distracted at work and colleagues and seniors would be disappointed with her. Also, her energy would be running her. She responded by jabbing me with a fork repeatedly on my upper thigh. Let's leave it there and look at Girl No. 3. Her problem is a little different. By this time, I had enough with non-empathetic women, so I decided to date a fellow astrologer. You must have heard of Gayatri Behen whose book, *Rahu Never Called Back* has been made into a super duper hit film in Tamil Nadu? Well, Gayatri Behen and I got along famously at first. Our predictions were also similar. But one day, on the day of my birthday, things started to go a little wrong. And that's because she actually presumed she was a better astrologer than me. And remember, a week before that, I had predicted that she would predict this prediction next. Back to my birthday, 19 May 1964. I'm a Taurean. And I had planned a big party at home, seventy-four people had RSVP-d. But, of course I knew that before the RSVPs. On the birthday morning, Gayatri Behen came to me and said that she wanted to cancel the party. Her readings showed, 'Tension with family members is on the cards. And not a good day for celebration and romance.' My readings showed, 'Great day for socializing, something special awaits you.' Anyhow, she was right. The party was a disaster. Heavy rains meant only nine people showed up. And three of them were the upset. My charts say to get a professional opinion on internal conflicts. But they are very expensive. And these guys don't allow you to smoke during the consultation, so I've no choice but to turn to you. Any ideas on how to balance the star charts, and the love life? If you can offer some practical and sane advice, I'll send you a copy of *Rahu Never Called Back*. After she left it behind, and never called back, I have little use for it now.

Sincerely,
Award Winning Astrologer

Dear Award Winning Astrologer,

I'd love to help you, but have been stopped by my astrologer to do so. You may remember her? Gayatri Behen? Extremely sorry about this, but it's beyond my control. By the way, Gayatri Behen says she doesn't want her copy *Rahu Never Called Back*! Please keep it with you, but don't change the ending.

Yours sincerely,
Award Winning Astrologer, myself
Lions Club of Matunga West
Little Lions Lower Club L.B.G. (Marg)

believe that in your book, *Your Wife Arranged My Marriage*, you have explained all the rules in the arranged marriage universe. I tried ordering a copy, but due to poor sales, (only seventeen copies were ever sold), the book has been discontinued. After harassing your publisher, and with the help of two bookshop owners, three raddiwallas, I was able to trace the owners of the seventeen sold copies. All seventeen addresses are the same. Yours! So basically since you have all the copies, I need to simply get back to you. Instead of going through the trouble of sending me a book, I thought it would be easier for you to, in brief, clear a few of my doubts. Here are my queries. Please note, they are not in any order of importance, but you can answer them in a rather hierarchical order, if you want to. Question A: Is it safe to have an arranged marriage? Question B: When you go to visit a prospective bride, are you allowed to touch her? Question C: Shouldn't both parties have a taste of physical relationship, to test the waters before consent? That's what we'd do if were buying a car, and shouldn't we treat this relationship at least on par, with the one with the car? Question D: Shouldn't the family provide a list of those she's been intimate with before, along with their personal information (like Facebook profiles and not, can one be provided to her on short notice? Question G: Is it okay if she verifies if she can swim? And if so, can she provide her list of preferred swimsuits, with her inside them? Question H: And the more generic questions, like her flexibility? Her food habits? Her relationship with plants? Her take on Communism? Her stand on Transfat? Her reaction to beggars at traffic lights? Her list of friends? And is she for or against MSG in Chinese food? Cell towers in the neighbourhood? And her stand on Honey Singh or Baba Saigal's Punjabi Rap contributions? Finally, should she not provide me with a detailed glimpse into her take on walking, talking, parking, and the blatant use of umbrellas, when there is a zero possibility of rain? Please, answer in a clinical unprejudiced manner. I remain your fan, although, if I must be honest, let me confirm that I'm still researching about you on the internet. Answer quickly please, my parents want an answer by Thursday. Thursday of which week though, is yet to be decided.

Yours sincerely,
Mr Protein Fibre

Dear Mr Protein Fibre,

The answer to all your question is no, no, yes, maybe,

both a complex and constantly evolving one. The secret to its success is the same as that of a love marriage. Though obviously the bride will be different in the two cases. These secrets include the four-fold path to harmony. The first part says spend as little time possible together on a daily basis. Since you'll be stuck together for years, please space out the commitment from the onset. The second part says avoid all personal remarks, both good and bad. You never say 'Her breath is awful', even though you are actually puking at that juncture. Conversely you never say, 'You are beautiful'. If you set this high standard, you'll have to pay for it. You'll have to repeat this line, every day of your life, forever. This makes no sense on two levels. One, if you outlive her and two, if she outlives you. Besides, no one can look beautiful over many, many years. In most marriages (love or arranged), beauty fades by the second weekend! However, your heart seems to be in the right place. And from the tone of your letter, I can sense that you've understood the main aim of marriage. And obviously, this aim has been around from time immemorial. Or at least, since June 1964. And that aim is to safeguard yourself. Yes that's right, marriage is about safeguarding oneself. It's a commitment between you and

and marriage. I think it would not be out of place for you to try your hand at both, i.e., an arranged marriage and a love marriage simultaneously before setting on settling one or the other. Remember, marriage is not about the journey. It's in fact, about the damn destination, and how you survive it. Let me know what you decide to do, so I can send you a list of prospective caterers.

Yours sincerely,
Cyrus

♥

Why are women so mean? My name is Sudhalakshmi. Some people think that's a girl's name, but it isn't. At least, not in my case. Today I'm twenty-one years old and girls have laughed at my expense for the last ten years of my life. But that's not the bad part. Worse is still to come. At my place of work, people are in the habit of hugging when they greet each other. There are nine ladies, and fourteen gents in our office. All the gents get hugs from the ladies, I alone get a handshake, or sometimes just a nod. Every time I go to hug a lady, I find nobody there.

23½ Ways to Make a Girl Fall For You

Dear Mr Indian,

First, let me apologize on not writing to you sooner. I tired. I mean I tried. But after seeing that picture, I needed three weeks recovery time. I still haven't recovered fully. It's affecting my grammar. I'm ending too many sentences with prepositions as a consequence of this ordeal. I know they say all are beautiful in God's eyes, but there has to be a limit. That a person with such a visage, can walk around freely is far beyond the cannon of democratic thought. I showed the picture to my neighbour, He's now moved to Canada. In four days! Canada!! Usually getting a Canadian Visa takes a month. But see what the human mind is capable off under the right duress, or motivation. Yet every cloud has a silver lining, goes the maxim unfortunately. In your case that won't hold true, sorry. Rarely, very rarely in the history of human romantic endeavour, do we come across a case which has broken through all barriers of genetics and horrid aesthetics. Presently hugging from any other human form seems far, far away. They also say there is someone for everyone. But if you try and contact the person who said that, you discover they are unavailable and untraceable. I myself am writing this letter to you from keep working on it, whilst staying far, far away from that photograph. I'm reading and re-reading the Greats from Kahlil Gibran to the biography of Olympian Champion Gymnast Mary Lou Retton. I'm hopeful of some good news in the time to come. Hang in there, but avoid any form of reproduction, till we get back to you with some

Yours truly,
Cyrus

♥

Now let's examine this letter from Anand Balakrishnan

I am Anand Balakrishnan from Madurai. My friends call me Bala. So you please call me Anand. Of course, if you call me Anand, I won't be able to respond to you, unless we are present physically, in close contact with one another. Which is not possible, as I am in Madurai, and I'm told you are in Mumbai. Why don't you give me your travel dates when you are next expected in Madurai? Here is my we don't talk much, we are always indulging in physical contact. Let me give you three examples. Last Tuesday our elbows bumped into one another while writing notes during the History class. I got so excited that I spelt Chandragupta's name with a 'w'. 'Guptaw'! On Thursday, I asked her for a pencil and our fingers touched. My finger is still tingling a whole week later. But, yesterday was even better! I said something funny, and she slapped my back, twice, and very hard. I can show you the mark when you are next in Madurai, or I'm in Mumbai (which is any time after October 2026). Do you think she likes me as much as I like her? Should I proceed?

Yours sincerely,
Anand.

My reply as usual was well thought out and to the point.

Let me be very frank here and tell you that your arguments to proceed with the relationship are highly misplaced. And proceeding would be, in my opinion, completely disastrous. Your examples are less solid, than an earthworm at birth. To make this more abundantly clear, let's call this such a touch can only be considered deliberate if it lingered for eight whole seconds, which it could only have done if she had passed out at the time. That brings us to the slapping your back incident. This act is actually the worst offense, as generally it's indulged by people of the same gender. Which translates to the possibilities that either she thinks you are a woman, or thinks of herself as a man. Either way, it's not to your advantage. So from what I can see the evidence is slim to nothing, and I'm just being really positive here. I suggest you wait for stronger cues, like long eye-contact, or her asking you out, before you proceed to the next step. But I do have some good news for you. Chandragupta, can be spelt, with a 'w' as it's a proper noun. Also, coincidentally from October 2026, I'll be travelling a lot for my work, so I'll have to get back to you on the dates. Madurai is also not on the radar for now. But let's go ahead, and stay in touch without actually meeting. For Lavanya, I'd suggest to you the opposite, i.e., meet, but don't touch.

Yours sincerely,
Cyrus Broacha

♥

sexual feelings towards my colleague Deepali and Priyanka. It's got so bad that I have totally stopped washing my hands at work. Last week was the office's anniversary, and we were fed cakes, *dosas* and *upmas* and *chutney* sandwiches. On such days one needs to wash one's hands desperately. Even after numerous toilet visits I avoid washing my hands. Is there any cure for me?

Yours expectantly,
Dibankar Sengupta

Dear Dibankar,

Honestly? No! You may visit a psychiatrist, but I doubt he could help you either. There seems to be only one avenue left for you to pursue. Okay, maybe two. One, you can get Deepali and Priyanka to leave the office and work somewhere else. Two, have you given any thoughts to wiping instead? If not paper, then passerby's pants.

Yours regretfully,
Cyrus Broacha

♥

last four years. However, last August she moved to Ohio University, and on her return the problems began. She cut her hair real short and now looks exactly like my seventeen-year-old cousin, Vivek. She also changed her name to Sam. Worst of all, she has this strange accent, which isn't really an American accent. It starts out like an Amricanish accent, then seems a little Bengali-meets-American, and finally it's a hybrid accent of a native of Hauz Khaus, schooled in Calcutta, and now studies in Ohio. Every time she rolls her R's I cringe in fear and pain. If I talk to her longer than five minutes I get a migraine. Every sentence now ends with a 'Yeah!' Can you imagine even when her answer is a simple 'Yeah', she follows it up with another 'Yeah', for cover. Last week, I asked her a really simple question. 'Do you want to go see a movie?' Her answer was, 'No, yeah!' So I asked her to clarify. 'Is it no or yeah?' Her reply you ask? 'It's a no yeah'. So in complete exasperation I asked her, 'Would that be no, or a yes?' Her carefully, clearly thought out reply was, that it's a 'No yeah, yeah!' At which point I may have thrown up, but I can't be sure because I think I also blacked out. This accent thing is driving me mad. I feel like avoiding her, even though I still love her. Please advise me on this

23½ Ways to Make a Girl Fall For You

Dear Naa-val (hope I got that right),

To answer your question, I can and I will. All of us know at least one colleague or neighbour who goes for a vacation to the United States, and comes back with a fake twang! Why do they do that? Probably because an accent is free. Not to mention you don't have to check it in at customs. And, mind you, this phenomenon only seems to occur when one is visiting the United States. I mean, I knew a couple who spent a year in the Fiji Islands and came back with even worse sounding original Indian accents, than they ever had before! What I'm trying to say is this brother—I feel your pain. And this bad, fake, horrendous half accent thing is definitely right up there with halitosis, body odour, and communism as a complete, serious turn-off. Now, about the commiseration. Let's give a call to action. Since I have felt this turmoil personally, let me share with you my strategy. This is based on the Professor Endid Papanicoulous Theory of Direct Reproach as espoused by him in his monumental work for the University of Athens, which was titled, 'Direct Reproach, As Espoused By Me For The University of Athens'.

that particular day would be bra-less. Luckily, Naval, (or should I write Naa-vul), in your specific situation, the Direct Reproach Theory works perfectly, starting tomorrow. I want you to try an accent of your own. For good ones you can try Peter Seller's character Hrundi V. Bakshi's accent in the film *The Party*. Or Did you mean Steven Seagal's accent, in any movie or interview. Or Bollywood celebrities doing interviews in English. Or even worse, Bollywood celebrities speaking in Hindi, while doing interviews in English. Let her have a taste of this bitter medicine. And do not, I repeat, do not stop until she brings up the matter. Trust me, the Direct Reproach Theory works like a charm.

All the Best, lots of luck,

Cyrus

♥

My name is not Something Wadhwa. It is Something Else Wadhwa. But I can't tell you what it is, because I'm quite well known in my industry. Which is not exactly an industry, but a bit more like a trade. The reason I can't tell

23½ Ways to Make a Girl Fall For You

My publicist says ten, but frankly it's a question of the pot calling the kettle black, as she would lose fifteen kilos herself. The problem is that I'm in love with my paternal aunt. I'm twenty-seven years old and she's forty-nine. She responds well to me, but I'm scared to pop the question. I want to know when is the right time to pop it? Also, what should I say? And do you think I need to give her some hints about my intentions first? And can you suggest what I should wear for this event, and do you think I should have my friend Karan stand by as a witness? Keep in mind that I have never been rejected before in my life. I'm very popular, and a household name. My chachi and I talk for hours. Mostly about our shared passion for fashion and food. We SMS each other twenty times a day. She's stunning and also well-known, as we are in the same industry. I mean trade. Please don't talk to me about morality, as I know at least seventeen different cultures in our country alone that approve of such blood relations. I can't ask my family for advice, so I turned to you. Please help! If things turn out well, I'll send you my autograph on my photograph, as I'm famous in my trade.

Yours sincerely,
Something Else Wadhwa

want to lose such a rare and precious keepsake. Now, there's no need to get defensive about your situation. You are not the last Indian man to get affected by intimate thoughts about older relatives, and you weren't the first either, third or fourth maybe, but not the first. Your point about seventeen sub-cultures having the answers to this question of morality is well-made, well-intentioned, and completely useless, pointless and absolutely futile. You see, that's only the second question in your argument. And it makes no sense getting to it until we scale the first major fundamental question. To which if the answer is no then this whole issue becomes totally redundant. Now I implore you to get your laptop or pen and paper, and answer this all important opening query about your romantic interlude. Does this elderly paternal aunt figure love you? And by love, I mean in the romantic and active way in which Tom Cruise once loved Penelope Cruz. The love that Elton John has for his partner David, what's his name? The love that Shia LaBeouf has for that paper bag on his head, etc. etc. It is not clear from your letter about her intentions or purpose.

Remember, just hanging out together doesn't automatically qualify for love. The Israelis and Palestinians would emit the required smell, telling one another of the other's intentions. Sadly, for human beings, as we age this smell is covered by other more odious smells, which lead to both confusion and possible retching.

If you could find out her intentions, we could then possibly look at question number two, and answer you better about your romantic future.

Thanks,
Cyrus

♥

I'm Jaco from Hungary. I'm an eighteen-year-old exchange program student. I have a bit of a cultural ignorance that I need help with. No Indian girl likes to look at me, or make eye contact. I've started to feel really ugly. Back in Budapest I was considered a good catch. But here they continuously look away, when I try to start a conversation. I started using Hamam soap, even though I couldn't stand the aroma. (Another cultural eye-opener). But, since I know my friend Naresh uses that soap, and has a girlfriend, I thought it was worth a punt. I also find that they are in our college. However, Naresh assured me it is not so. Could you please help me? I'm told you have dedicated your life to solving cultural disparities.

Thanking you,
Jaco

I would say 'Welcome to India'. But, it's obviously too late. Along with your malaria and dysentery shots, Europeans must be given a crash course in Indian cultural peculiarities. Before I attend to your specific problem, allow me to give you few general examples. In most Indian cities, pedestrians walk on the roads during traffic. This is normal, almost customary. Our pavements are used only by pigeons. Also, the normal and the customary. Recently our pavements have been overrun by two-wheelers. Sadly, this may dispense the pigeons. And this will soon be the new normal, by all accounts. Of course, the pigeons could simply join the vehicles, public and mosquitoes on our roads. All and everything is welcome there.

Now, it seems like your Hungarian Rhapsody isn't quite working in India. Don't be alarmed, you are not the first European to struggle with the local ladies. Sir many years it was only practiced amongst males. I won't bore you with details, but a lot of it has to do with the fact that we still are a disease-riddled nation. And oral transmission of diseases is still a big problem, especially amongst unrelated, educated people of the opposite gender. So here's who you can kiss in India—pets, cows, religious symbols, the heavens, your hand, and your other hand. Stick to this and you will be safe.

And about the eye-contact issue, 74 per cent of Indian males suffer from an inability to blink, especially when looking at women. The only time they blink is when you ask them about their future plans. Women don't like staring at these men, or being stared at by these men for a number of, but not restricted to reasons, such as: (1) Indian men can look strange, (2) they do weird things with their eyeballs, (3) they often bang into cars while staring at girls, (4) they have their mouths open simultaneously whilst staring. Thus, creating a breeding ground for diseases.

Jaco, enjoy India, but approach both men and women from afar. If I was you, I'd have done that from Budapest, but that's different story.

Cyrus

peri cardial cover

Let's now move forward, by going a couple of steps sideways to the margin of this page. It's time to open the perimeter, increase the boundary rope and widen the horizons. After using the collective will of all my pets and employees in uniform, I have discovered points from beyond the pale. No love almanac is complete without them. Dear Lover, please commit all points to memory. Then never speak of them in public ever again!

Let us now turn to the official Indophile scholar and most importantly, winner of the Harikrishna Das Mansukbhai Banjatya award (2012)—Mr Edward Gills the 3rd. Mr Gills the , who likes to be called by his suffix, 3rd (to be pronounced 'The Third') had dedicated his life to studying the romantic behaviour of the Indian male. How he got to this grouping is of immense interest. A zoologist by training, 3rd initially studied the life of the people of Kwala Zulu Natal. However, since he derogatory word, and hence is much happier with the more classy home relative 'ass'. Although 3rd's digestive system withstood the Indian culinary assault he ran out of Ass by day four of his studies. As John Lennon says, 'Life is what happens to you while you are busy making other plans'. And so, 3rd while focusing on the Indian ass stumbled upon the Indian male. Firstly, he was actually able to make the distinction. Secondly, he started finding the latter's behaviour more fascinating than the former. For six months he followed the Indian male, surviving only on cans of baked beans the whole time just to be safe. He jotted down with pictures all his findings. Then he put all that into an 11,637 page journal. To condense his findings is a monumental task. But I managed to overcome that. To start, I simply ignored his first 900 pages and collected all my information from the remaining ones. So here are the unadulterated vows on arguably the foremost and possibly only scholarly account of the subject: 'Romantic practices of the Indian male'.

> I find the Indian male to be a captivating study. He gave me more trouble than all the South African tribes put together. And he defiantly was more socially awkward than the infamous Wild Ass, who would often eat tit and bits from my hand. Something the Indian male

before meals. What was more fascinating was that, in spite of cutlery being readily available he used the same hands for eating all his meals as well. He later also informed me of all the other things he did with his hands. Appalling things. Quite unmentionable, so much so that I started buying him Dettol soaps for the same hands but for my own safety. This peculiar behavioural pattern was mesmerizing to the western academia and so I started observing Mahendra and his ilk, and uncovered some startling information.

The Indian male, and more specifically the lesser-educated Indian male's attitude towards the opposite sex is based solely upon one attribute or quality. And that is a complete ignorance about scientific terms! It's like Donald Trump holidaying in Mexico with Sarah Palin Mahendra informed me that until he was married off to his wife at the age of twenty-two (she was eighteen), he had never seen a naked woman in his life. This is alien and contrary to the western way, where it is only after marriage that a man rarely gets to see the female naked form again. He also added that at their first meeting, his wife and he sat beside each other like two inanimate objects for about two-and-a-half hours. So he was greatly a bit possessive, but only about his cattle. He initially didn't like his wife interacting with his precious buffalo. Now of course, he's far more enlightened and allows such interactions as long as it's restricted to not more than twice a week and between the timings of nine and eleven in the morning, and never on weekends. When I quizzed him on his wife, I got this surprising group of answers which I must share in its fullness.

: Mahendra, when is your wife's birthday?

M: I think on Wednesday.

3rd: What are her favourite hobbies?

M: I think Thursday.

3rd: Who has been her biggest inspirations?

M: Then say like that no, it will be Wednesday.

3rd: How would you please her? What makes her

M: I will ask her mother, but not now.

3rd: Then when?

M: Wednesday.

For this interview, which took place over five days, I found that Mahendra really needed to look beyond Thursday, and after seven years of marriage had not progressed an inch. Not an iota or regard to information from their perspective this ignorance card therefore may not be irrational as it first seemed. And the only receiving accepted western trends. Lack of information and interest may be the cornerstone of longevity in marriages. As proven by the higher survival rate of middle-India marriages vis-à-vis pan America marriages! Time to rest my case.

It is difficult to trace the genesis of the Indian male's misguided journey in pursuit of female companionship. Of course, his misguided journey in pursuit of male companionship can be traced to Hindi movies of the 70s and the 80s. Going back to the first point we can argue for hours, but since I can't hear you let's just go with my point. There are many theories on the origin of this aforementioned misguidance. But, the following theory is what makes most sense and I can verify this by informing you that I found this theory at the back of a Chinese takeaway menu card in Shanghai last year.

Around 1220 A.D., when Genghis and his band of merry men were attacking the Jin Empire of Northern China (the Gin Empire gave us the fabulous Gin chicken recipe which goes down very well with chilli sauce and a hint of mint), four Indian spice merchants were caught in

The merchants won over the Tangut hearts with their invention of doors. Yes, doors! The Tanguts who lived in tents hadn't yet discovered the concept of a door. Their tents were kept open on two sides, thus allowing insects, moose and wolves in, along with other pets like somebody else's husband. Doors changed the Tagut's way of life. Post-doors, their children started resembling their parents. Overjoyed with the Indian merchants, the Taguts shared the merchants' needs, as a gesture of good faith. When the merchants returned to India with all the goodwill and confidence, each of them founded a kingdom of their own where they each propagated the door culture to a fanatical level. This kept men and woman apart for the next seven centuries. Thus allowing reticence, shyness, awkwardness hypocrisy aggressiveness and frustration to creep into the Indian DNA. So, in a nutshell it's the fault of the Mongols and the only prudent thing to do is have our High Commissioner take this up with Ulan Bator's high Commissioner. And in keeping with international diplomatic traditions, whoever is higher wins.

Mind you this is one of the many theories—377 in all. I hereby promise to look at 249 of them in this book alone. Okay, you're

This theory comes from leading Bollywood actor Varun Dhawan, who has said on record that women are secretly running this country. This was said in an ad campaign for women empowerment called the 'Power of 49'. To authenticate his comment, we reviewed the ad eighty-four times and matched his voice and mannerisms from his performance in a film *Student of the Year*. My findings were jaw-dropping. But, since I can't recall them let's go with the fact that this authenticated his comment, if time gives credence to the Indian male's awkwardness, shyness and all-round misguided infantile behaviour around women. For example, a male who sulks around a girl while the poor girl doesn't even know he exists in the first place. Well, such behaviours would make a lot of sense if women had ruled men in the original equation. Thus, women learned to ignore their subjects. The subjects, in turn, were unable to communicate or make any impression on their males. There's much more to this theory than is blatantly obvious.

The other day I was stunned when a seven-year-old boy asked me to help him 'patao girls'? I was even more stunned because he was choking me simultaneously, while politely asking me this question. After restraining him with the help of his volume levels, I could not hear him, nor he me, nor Rigoletto either of us. So I did the next best thing. I researched the lives and love techniques of ten of India's most famous lovers, the Don Juans, even perhaps the Lotharios. It was an exhaustive process as all ten don't live in the same house. I was able to glean important information though a commonality of qualities that the ten possessed. I have, for all the reasons of security, privacy and defamation, changed the names of all ten. Better still, I've decided not to name any of them at all by name. Instead, all references to the concerned ten will be done with a wink and an obligatory nod.

Nine out of the chosen ten were extremely hygienic. Flossing was more important than brushing. Yet, whitening of the teeth, especially among those over thirty, was quite a common occurrence. For eight of these love champions, hair was immaculate. Hair products like mousse gel and heavenly-smelling oils were studied and applied judiciously. Attention to eyebrows, eyelashes, nose hair, ear hair, earwax, sideburns and beards was paramount. They worked hard on their looks as women unlike other men paid attention to detail. The Slavs have a saying: An earhair would cost you a marriage/ It doesn't stop their landscaping across the body of course. Bodies were also in some sort of shape, although the Indian man's shape itself is questionable. Huge attention was given to the smell. A good aroma seems to usher in a sense of romance, acceptance and availability. Keep in mind that over 85 per cent of animals doors, letting the lady sit first, not leaving your jeans zipper open during a date in public, etc., also seems to be part of this tribe's mantra.

However, in all this, one very important point is that those ten men, beautiful as they are, never try to out-beauty the women they are with, implying that it is nice to be well-groomed but never over-groomed. Well-groomed is symbolic of success. Out-grooming the lady is a recipe for disaster. My thanks to Kunal, Vikram, Sameer, Parag, Rustom, Neal, Manek, Rajeev, Sanjay and Mohit. Sorry, shouldn't have used their names. Oops!

the 'gum' method

It is time to open our eyes to some tried and tested attempts by our brethren (and I'm using that term very loosely), to successfully create an aura for themselves, which causes a profound positive effect on woman-kind. Men have disguised themselves, or rather taken on various avatars in order to successfully seduce or captivate women, since the time man domesticated the Tyrannosaurus Rex, in a mistaken belief, that all dinosaurs were just grown-up horses.

In Latin America, Ralph Herrandez Coutto used to disguise himself as a fruit (mostly as a grand papaya), in order to ingratiate himself with ladies. He was successful until someone decided to cut him up and serve him during one misguided Easter banquet. In modern day Estonia, Vaclad the First successfully pretended to be a statute outside a working woman's hostel. He produced eighty-nine children. And more importantly, paid roots can be traced to the Mohenjo-daro and Harappan building societies. It is from those halcyon days of yore, that the 'Gum' method has been practiced, to woo the 'ladies'.

The 'Gum' method basically entails a person of divine nature (this divinity generally determined by the man himself), who uses spirituality as a weapon to 'triumph' with girls. And by triumph, I don't mean that every time he's successful he jumps up and down, delirious with joy, arms akimbo. Although, this has been the traditional reaction amongst 'Gums' 17 per cent of the time. The 'Gum' process is simple:

> Decide you are a 'Gum'.
> Tell everyone you are a 'Gum'.
> Stop Shaving.
> Give up wearing innerwear.

The only complications is this 'avtaar', is that you must have working knowledge of spirituality, so this knowledge of spirituality is important. As women are enticed in the 'Gum', the rest is easy. Poor growth of facial hair and the wrong colour robes are the only pitfalls of this trade. At least two Swami's with their transparent attires, for instance, failed in their endeavours to lure the opposite sex.

The 'Gum' method has been expanded and evolved in

The publishers of this book as well as the author, and three of his youngest relatives must adhere that they neither endorse nor advocate the 'Gum' method. We are just allowing you a glimpse into your own tradition and history, which is richly laden, and embellished with many jewels, such as the 'Gum'

Please don't Google 'el concludo', it may or may not be a Spanish word. I heard it first being used by a four-year-old on a bus going toward Churchgate railway station, and bear in mind the boy was sneezing at the time as well. Please take it up with him. And frankly, I did experiment with other words, but 'finito' and 'kaput' didn't have the same feel. Also 'el 'diablo' made no sense whatsoever. Yet, both I and my publishers (one of whom has quit the business after reading this book), felt the reader must have some conclusion. After all, I may have promised some sort of solutions to love problems, specifically regarding 'patoing' the fairer sex. These promises I, of course, deny immediately. But before that, we examine the ideas and inspirations that gave rise to what can be seen as a noble piece of work, in very backward cultures that lived, long, long ago. Or maybe a little longer than that!

when the men's public urinal has been too dangerous to negotiate. However, for the most part I've been a card-carrying member of the Indian male brotherhood.

Across the length and breadth of this great public, I have noticed lots of issues which are exclusively male. From what I call 'male pattern baldness', to smelling your own armpit, to staring at the other gender, oblivious to the hostility that such an act may breed. I myself have slipped, stumbled, and fallen over in many haphazard attempts to engage the fairer sex. Once, I entered the ladies toilet of the famous Sophia College (where my mother and wife once studied though not at the same time) by mistake, only to be chased out by, shall we say, a holy person. It was a genuine mistake, caused by the habitual problem of assuming that a left is a right, and a right is a left. Others, who are geographically challenged, will comprehend my anguish, as it were. The daggers I got in terms of looks from the college girls around only meant that it took about six months before I could make eye contact with the opposite sex again. My point, which I've gradually eroded, is that having walked in the shoes of the socially-challenged-male, I understand our 'problems', and am able to vaguely offer a helping hand after years of trying to climb errr…the…errr… insurmountable mountain. The challenges we males face remain me toe nails are part of personal hygiene. They are not. They are too low down in the scheme of things to warrant the 'personal hygiene' attention.

By sharing these stories of the brave, intrepid lovers-to-be (who dauntlessly and dumb-founded, tread sloppily into the dark night), I'm hoping to get our brotherhood to identify with the issues at hand, confront their own devils, and occasionally win their maiden's fair hand. And, when they don't succeed, I don't want them to cry like babies and call their mothers. I can tell you from past experiences that after a few times, a mother's phone can quite suddenly have an engaged tone. Worse, it's accompanied by Engelbert Humpledink songs like 'Leaving on a Jet Plane', which only serves to accelerate the problem.

Males, I reach out to you. Please reach out to me. But, maintain distance and don't make physical contact, because even the 'love jungle' has its rules. This concludes, 'el concludo'. Worry not if you can't make out head or tail, my next book, coming soon, will explain everything. I think.

LOVE ON!!!!!!!!!!!

www.ingramcontent.com/pod-product-compliance
Lightning Source LLC
Chambersburg PA
CBHW030233170426
43201CB00006B/209

9788129139573